COM
BUSINESS PHRASES

COMMON JAPANESE BUSINESS PHRASES

Compiled by
Sanseido

Translated and adapted by
John Brennan

Misa Miyachi

KODANSHA INTERNATIONAL
Tokyo · New York · London

Distributed in the United States by Kodansha America, Inc., 114 Fifth Avenue, New York N.Y. 10011, and in the United Kingdom and continental Europe by Kodansha Europe Ltd., 95 Aldwych, London WC2B 4JF. Published by Kodansha International Ltd., 17-14 Otowa 1-chome, Bunkyo-ku, Tokyo 112-8652, and Kodansha America, Inc.

First edition, 1998
98 99 00 10 9 8 7 6 5 4 3 2 1
ISBN 4-7700-2299-9

CONTENTS

Preface

The Japanese language encompasses a remarkably elaborate inventory of entrenched, often idiomatic, conventional phrases —phrases which tend to evade the grasp of people not privy to the whole code or accustomed to the situations in which that code applies. Nowhere is this more true than in the Japanese working world, where real communication (as opposed to communication of the ceremonial or purely formal variety) tends to be framed in concise if not elliptical units and where the best kind of understanding is invariably an implicit one. In a working culture where standard business phrases, laden with implications quite beyond the reach of the uninitiated, are bandied about like badminton birdies, the hapless non-native will be left watching from the sidelines unless she or he can get some solid guidance on how and when some of the more important phrases are used. That's what this book is for: to provide readers of English who work in the Japanese business world with a set of highly practical and socially appropriate standard Japanese expressions for use on the job or in related situations, as well as an account of the sorts of situations in which these expressions will be most useful.

To get an idea of how and why this particular selection of common business phrases came to be presented—the list offered here is far from exhaustive—and to understand the specific perspective from which these recommendations on usage issue, it will help to know something of this book's origins.

In 1992 the publishing firm Sanseido put out a Japanese-language volume entitled *Kimari Monku no Jiten,* or "Dictionary of Common Phrases." It's not really a dictionary, but a handbook of language etiquette. As such, it was apparently intended for the edification of younger Japanese readers (rather younger than the authors, that is) whose formal schooling might have prepared them to build a better mouse pad but very likely did not, at least in the authors' estimation, equip them with the language sensibilities needed to negotiate routine social formalities—answering the phone, presenting someone with a gift, apologizing for an indiscretion—with the requisite level of politeness and decorum. To rectify these inadequacies and provide new generations of Japanese speakers with the means to conduct themselves in a duly genteel and socially accommodating manner, *Kimari Monku no Jiten* offered a catalogue of standard phrases recommended for use in particular situations.

In surprising numbers (surprising to some people, surely), whole ranks of the youth of Japan seem to accept—or at least entertain the notion—that they need specific guidance from their elders on how to speak their own native language in order to qualify as phraseologically upright, etiquette-savvy, grown-up members of society. That, at any rate, would be one way to interpret the wide readership enjoyed by language-improvement books such as Sanseido's *Kimari Monku no Jiten.* Some or most of this apparent concern for learning to mind one's language doubtless arises from the anxiety a lot of young people feel about entering the work force and the pressing need to possess all the right tools for success in business; one essential tool, it turns out, is a facility for employing all the right businesslike expressions when on the job. To address this specific need, *Kimari Monku no Jiten* included an extensive list of phrases especially suitable for use by business people, reflecting above all the particular concerns and specialized environments of Japanese corporate culture.

The Sanseido book caught the eye of the editors of Kodansha International's Power Japanese series, who realized that, with certain modifications, a guide to Japanese language etiquette—even one originally written for native speakers—would have much to offer advanced students of the language and might hold appeal for other readers as well, including people not quite so far along in their study of Japanese. And so it came about that, in 1996, I was commissioned to transform the contents of Sanseido *Kimari Monku no Jiten* into something more comprehensible (or at least more presentable) to readers of English. The first fruits of this undertaking, comprising a slightly scaled-down catalogue of Japanese phrases for use in everyday life, were published last year under the title *Common Japanese Phrases* (1997, Kodansha International). The volume before you, dealing with the business end of things, represents the completion of the task.

This book, like its predecessor, was put together with two different group of readers in mind. The first group consists of people who already have a pretty firm grasp of the mechanics of Japanese grammar and the basics of usage, who are familiar with the structural inflections associated with various levels of polite, honorific, and humble language, and who have acquired a more or less functional Japanese vocabulary. None of these points is explicitly addressed here; they're covered by books of the sort that serious students have probably already read. Readers who do have a basic grounding in the language—or who are way beyond the basics—will find whole great chunks of highly useful phraseology here to fill gaps in or lend authenticity to the command of Japanese they already possess, as well as a wealth of insights and observations regarding the social and psychological contexts that help determine judgments about appropriate usage.

The other group whose interests this book will serve is made up of people who don't know any Japanese to speak of and aren't about to tackle the whole project now. These readers might be looking for some handy phrases to toss off around the office or in the boardroom, enabling them to take people by surprise or keep the opposition off balance or make their Japanese colleagues wonder how much they really understand. There's plenty in these pages to suit those purposes, too, with the added benefit of explanations of the responses these phrases can ordinarily be expected to elicit.

As for the translation itself, I've tried to put everything into natural-sounding American English, foregoing any literal decoding of the components of a phrase or sentence in favor of a faithful rendering of the sense or meaning of the whole. To some extent I've tried to approximate in English the degree of formality, politeness, or self-deprecation that's explicit in the Japanese, but I'll only have succeeded in those cases where the reader's sense of these elusive qualities happens to coincide with my own. The conventions for transliterating Japanese are those observed in the other books in the Power Japanese series.

The pages of this book are replete with suggestions, exhortations, and admonitions to employ this expression rather than that one in order to achieve a certain result in a given circumstance. Taken together, these prescriptions reflect a distinctive outlook on language and human interaction, not to mention the business world, that originates with the authors of the original work of which this is a translation, not with me. I've done what I could to inject a little levity here and there as a means of counterbalancing some of the more strident pronouncements in the original text, but anybody who's looking for a surefire line to bring down the house in a roomful of Japanese executives is entirely on his or her own.

***

Once again, I'm very grateful to Michael Brase of Kodansha

International for preserving an enthusiasm for the project during that dark wait before the dawn. I'm also grateful to KI's Shigeyoshi Suzuki for his comments and assistance. Deepest thanks to Kaori Yashiro for precious aid and inspiration and to Iku Nonaka for her unflagging encouragement, and many thanks again and always to the great Tom Gally.

John Brennan

June 1998

まえがき

　言葉には、ただ字面の意味が分かってもどうにもならない種類の
ものがあります。使われる情況と非常に深くかかわり合っているた
め、それが分からなければどう分析しようがまったく歯が立たない
暗号のようなものがあります。この暗号性という意味で、まさにビ
ジネス界で使われる慣用表現ほど典型的なものはないかも知れませ
ん。使われるべき表現は場面により要領よく決められていて、いち
いち事細かに説明しなくても十分にコミュニケーションがはかれる
ようにセットされています。逆にいえば、セットされた約束事、ビ
ジネス習慣を知らなければ、言葉のやりとりを聞いていてもまるで
バドミントンのシャトルコックが右、左へ飛び交うのをただ呆然と
眺めているようなものになってしまうわけです。

　本書の目的は、日本のビジネス界ではどのような表現がどのよう
な場面において使われ、どのような内容、情報また心理や感情を伝
達するのか、そのルールを出来る限り明確に説明することにありま
す。本書のベースとなっているのは、三省堂が1992年に出版した
『決まり文句の辞典』。この本は辞典というより「ことばのエチケッ
トブック」といった観があり、本来日本人の若い読者に向けて書か
れたものです。上司や顧客に対する言葉遣い、ものを頼むとき、交
渉するとき、謝罪する場合といった具合に場面が具体的に設定され
ていて、敬語表現や礼節にかなった言い回し、あるいは相手を傷つ
けずにどうしたら自分の言いたいことが言えるのかなど懇切丁寧に
説明しています。

　それにしても、このような本が出版されること自体大変興味深い
現象と言わざるを得ません。日本語のネイティヴ・スピーカーにこ
れほどまで手取り足取り日本語を教えているのですから。しかしこ
れも考えてみますと無理なからぬ事情があるようです。若者たち自
身、先輩たちから「言葉遣い」を教えてもらわなければ、社会に出
てから困ると感じています。大人の世界でやっていくにはそれなり
の言葉遣いを知らなくては一人前にはなれないと思っているからです。

　このようなわけで、『決まり文句の辞典』を外国の日本語学習者用
に仕立て直すことは大変理にかなっていると考えられます。事実、

講談社インターナショナルでは日本語学習者向けのシリーズ「パワージャパニーズ」でこの辞典に基づき、『Common Japanese Phrases』(1997年) という慣用表現集を出版し、なかなかの評判を得ているようです。私もその出版をお手伝いしたひとりとして大変意を強くしている次第です。

さて本書の読者ですが、先の慣用句集同様ふたとおりの読者層を想定しています。ひとつは既にひととおり日本語学習を終えていて、文法事項なども頭に入っている学習者。ビジネス世界で頻繁にしかも機能的に使われる表現や情報を盛り込んだ本書はそれまで培った知識や経験に磨きをかけ、必ずや実践的ハンドブックとなるはずです。いまひとつの読者は、特に日本語はできないが日本人ビジネスマンと仕事をするチャンスがあり、日本のビジネス社会や習慣を少しでも知りたい、あるいは必要に応じて多少の日本語でも使ってみたいといった方々です。本書をひととおり読んでいただければ、日本のビジネス社会の輪郭が見えてくるはずです。

本書の翻訳については原則として自然なアメリカ英語を心がけ、字義ひとつひとつをなぞることをせずに全体の意味をくむ方向で進めました。また敬語表現の丁寧度についてはなるべく翻訳に反映させるよう努めました。その他表記全般については、パワージャパニーズのスタイルによっています。

本書には、言葉を使用する際の注意、忠告、助言がいっぱい詰まっています。これらは、いわば人間と言葉の観察から導き出された智恵とでも称すべきもので、ひとつビジネス界にとどまらず、ひろく日常の言語生活に応用できる処方箋といえるでしょう。このような立派な処方箋ができあがったのは、もちろん原著者の功績によるもので、私は少しばかり蛇足を加えさせていただいたに過ぎません。本書がみなさまのお役に立つことを心から願っています。

この本ができるまでには本当にいろいろな方のお力添えがありました。八代かおりさん、野中郁さんには貴重な意見やあたたかい励ましをいただき、講談社インターナショナルのマイケル・ブレイズ氏には辛抱強く私の遅筆につきあっていただき、同社の鈴木重好氏からも助言をいただきました。トム・ガリー氏には、いつもながら大変示唆に富むアドバイスを頂戴し深く感謝しています。この他お名前を省かせていただいた方々にも、こころより感謝申し上げます。ありがとうございました。

1998年6月
ジョン・ブレナン

My name's Brown.
How do you do?

初めましてブラウンと申します。

Hajimemashite Buraun to mōshimasu.

My name's Brown. How do you do?

The importance of making a good first impression is a well-established principle of business not only in Japan but throughout the world. Singularly emphatic importance, however, is attached to this point in the Japanese business world, where form is supremely important (and function often runs a distant second), so particularly close attention should be paid to proper introductions. Whenever you meet someone for the first time in your role as a working person, it's only proper and polite to introduce yourself. When you do so, you'll want to strike the right note of seriousness, formality, and confidence, for which purpose the standard phrase at the beginning of this section—properly delivered—will serve you well.

Note that only the surname is given. What's more, in this case a surname consisting of a single syllable in its original form weighs in at a hefty four syllables when rendered into Japanese: "BU-RA-U-N." To properly introduce yourself, you have to make sure that your name registers with the other party, which requires that you pronounce it the way it's rendered in the Japanese sound system (if you don't know, consult someone who does). This can be tricky, and it may take a good deal of practice before your own name rolls off your tongue the way it should in Japanese.

Should you ever feel like straying slightly from the well-beaten path, here's a less often heard, slightly longer variation to hold in reserve:

初めてお目にかかります。ブラウンと申します。

Hajimete ome ni kakarimasu. Buraun to mōshimasu.

How do you do? My name's Brown.

Strictly in terms of meaning, the expression *Hajimete ome ni kakarimasu* (literally, "I present myself before your eyes for the first time") carries the same message as "I don't believe we've met." In terms of usage, however, it's probably more useful to regard this as another way to say "How do you do?"

In business circles, individual identity is often less important than the matter of whom you represent, so it may be preferable to begin your introduction with that information:

初めましてヤマト商事のブラウンでございます。

Hajimemashite Yamato Shōji no Buraun de gozaimasu.

My name's Brown, with Yamato Trading. How do you do?

While the name of the individual appears first in the translation above (because that's the preferred order in English), in Japanese the name of the firm precedes that of the person introducing himself. Some might consider this difference to be emblematic of an essential contrast between the English-speaking and Japanese-speaking corporate cultures.

I'm sorry to bother you at a busy time

お忙しいところを恐れいります。

Oisogashii tokoro o osoreirimasu.

I'm sorry to bother you at a busy time.

One cherished assumption that features prominently in Japan's corporate culture, as well as in popular mythology, is the notion that Japanese business people always have far more work to do than time to do it in—that to be up to their ears in it every waking moment is their natural state. A self-serving image, perhaps, but one that is duly enshrined in office language and etiquette. Accordingly, unless you acknowledge at the outset that your visit, your call, your meeting, or even your phone message is keeping the other person from something far more important, you'll be starting out on the wrong foot. You can pay the necessary dues with the single phrase given above. Or you might try:

お忙しいところをお邪魔いたしまして……

Oisogashii tokoro o ojama itashimashite ...

Forgive me for intruding on your busy schedule.

For an especially formal business call, you might try more formal language:

わざわざお時間を割いていただきまして恐縮に
　存じます。

Wazawaza ojikan o saite itadakimashite kyōshuku ni zon-jimasu.

I'm very grateful to you for allowing me to impose on your time.

Seeing as how you're expected to apologize even for a scheduled business call, it's hardly a good idea to drop in on people without an appointment. As a rule, don't make unscheduled calls if you can avoid it. Should it somehow come about that you urgently need to see someone and don't have an appointment, you'll need to convince the other person that you'll keep it short. After apologizing for your intrusion, bid the absolute minimum:

15分で結構ですから……

Jūgo-fun de kekkō desu kara ...

If I could have just fifteen minutes of your time ...

Presuming this approach works, it's up to you to make sure you've spoken your piece by the time your fifteen minutes are up. The ability to do so is the mark of a pro, so you actually have an opportunity to transform what could have been an awkward disruption into a display of concision and efficiency. You can also help make a name for yourself as someone who knows and respects the value of time, which can only be to your advantage in the future.

In the business world, of course, keeping busy is everything; after all, what does "business" mean if not staying busy? When people are hard at work, money is being made and, presumably, profits are accumulating. In this sense, by indicating you know someone is very busy, you're subtly sending a very positive signal—the suggestion that this person is engaged in a vital, prosperous enterprise. There's a simple phrase that, while usually used in an offhand or even a euphemistic manner, succinctly conveys this compliment. Suppose that after arriving at a client's office for a scheduled meeting, you've been kept waiting. Finally your man turns up and apologizes:

大変お待たせしました。

Taihen omatase shimashita.

I'm really sorry to have kept you waiting.

Now, you could simply trot out a standard (and sadly unimaginative) retort:

どういたしまして。

Dō itashimashite.

Not at all.

Or you could seize the opportunity to toss off this timely line:

忙しそうで、なによりです。

Isogashisō de, nani yori desu.

You certainly seem to be busy—and that's what it's all about.

To get down
to the business at hand

さっそくですが……

Sassoku desu ga ...

To get down to the business at hand ...

When you call on a client or when someone calls on you, the conversation will invariably open with an exchange of greetings and politely innocuous inquiries about everyone's health, possibly augmented by commentary on the weather or the state of the economy. But sooner or later (and don't be deceived by all this leisurely politeness—sooner is usually better), someone has to broach the subject of business. The phrase above serves as an unmistakable signal that the preliminaries have been dispensed with and it's time to get down to business, as in:

さっそくですが、本日伺いましたのは……

Sassoku desu ga, honjitsu ukagaimashita no wa ...

To get down to the business at hand, the reason
    I'm here today is ...

With this utterance, the social formalities and polite chatter cease. It's on to business, and once the talk has taken this inevitable turn, pity the fool who wastes precious time trying to lighten the atmosphere with frivolous remarks. This is all the more true, of course, when the conversation is interrupting a particularly busy day, and in such a case it may be best to cut straightaway to the gist of the matter, using one of these phrases:

手短に申し上げます。
Temijika ni mōshiagemasu.
Let me sum up the situation for you.

かいつまんで申しますと……
Kaitsumande mōshimasu to ...
To make a long story short ...

When the topic at hand involves something that has already yielded a clear outcome, very often the best strategy is to open with that:

まず結論から申しますと……
Mazu ketsuron kara mōshimasu to ...
First let me give you the upshot.

Another useful opening strategy is to enumerate the items that need to be addressed:

二点ほどお伝えすることがございます。
Niten hodo otsutae suru koto ga gozaimasu.
There are just two things I'd like to go over with you.

By taking this approach you can reassure the other person that you won't be bending his ear for the rest of the afternoon, and at the same time you can effectively draw his attention to the specific points you're enumerating.

Now and then you might be compelled to broach a subject that you know the other person really doesn't want to address—and will try hard to avoid. If you simply launch into one of these conversational sore spots without warming up the audience a bit, you're all too likely to elicit an adverse response. The wisest policy is to ease into the subject gently by signaling that it's coming up:

そろそろ、例の件をお話ししたいと存じますが……

Sorosoro, rei no ken o ohanashi shitai to zonjimasu ga ...

Now then, I wonder if we could move on and maybe discuss that other matter.

I'd like to look into this and come back and try again

研究して出直してまいります。

Kenkyū shite denaoshite mairimasu.

I'd like to look into this and come back and try again.

A true professional doesn't abandon hope simply because her sales pitch was rejected or his presentation failed to persuade the audience. On the contrary, the real pro is distinguished by determination, persistence, and the ability to look beyond temporary setbacks toward the ultimate goal. Suppose you're trying to get someone to do business with you and find you've run up against a wall. You've reached the point where a lesser person would cut his losses and accept defeat with a meek apology:

お邪魔しました。

Ojama shimashita.

Sorry to have wasted your time.

Not for you a simpering surrender, however. For now, you'll fall back and regroup, but not before letting the other party know that you, like another old soldier who lost the battle only to win the war, shall return:

研究して出直してまいります。

Kenkyū shite denaoshite mairimasu.

I'd like to look into this and come back and try again.

With these words, you gracefully concede the present round and declare your intention to render satisfaction next time. Here's a slightly longer and more gracious way to accomplish the same thing:

貴重なご意見をありがとうございました。さっ そく研究いたしまして、あらためて出直して まいります。

Kichō na go-iken o arigatō gozaimashita. Sassoku ken-kyū itashimashite, aratamete denaoshite mairimasu.

Thank you for sharing your ideas—they're extremely helpful. We'll give this immediate and careful consideration, and I'll be back with a new proposal.

Here's another way to put the best possible face on a failed first attempt, this time somewhat less directly:

本日は大変勉強になりました。これをご縁に一
層努力いたしますので、今後ともよろしくご
指導ください。

Honjitsu wa taihen benkyō ni narimashita. Kore o goen ni issō doryoku itashimasu no de, kongo tomo yoroshiku goshidō kudasai.

Today's discussion has been extremely instructive. This is going to make me work even harder (to get your business), and I'd be very grateful to receive more of this kind of guidance in the future.

Having asserted your never-say-die attitude, you might, depending on the circumstances, try to pin down a date and time for your next sally. If the other side is agreeable, you're likely to hear something on the order of:

では来週にでもご連絡ください。

Dewa raishū ni demo gorenraku kudasai.

Okay then, contact us next week or so.

Nice going, you're still in the ballgame. But the other party could refuse to be pinned down, offering only a vague assurance that they'll be in touch:

いずれこちらからお電話します。

Izure kochira kara odenwa shimasu.

Either way, we'll give you a call.

Oh, well. Don't cancel all your appointments waiting for that call.

Remember, it takes time to put together a business arrangement. You shouldn't take yourself out of the game just because nobody has swung at your first couple of pitches. If you have the fire and tenacity to keep coming back at them, those qualities will ultimately tell the tale. That's when you may will hear these words, which will show you've carried the day:

いや、あなたの熱意には負けました。

Iya, anata no netsui ni wa makemashita.

Okay, okay, you've won me over.

Hello. Mr. Watanabe, of course

いらっしゃいませ、渡辺様でございますね。

Irasshaimase, Watanabe-sama de gozaimasu ne.

Hello. Mr. Watanabe, of course

Like it or not, a visitor's first impression of the organization you work for is apt to be determined by the reception he gets from the person who greets him upon his arrival. A polite, cheerful word of welcome—*irasshaimase*—will strike a perfectly cordial note with virtually any visitor and will help convey the impression that he's dealing with a first-rate outfit.

Generally, someone who has arrived to pay a business call will announce herself by stating the name of the firm she represents and her own name (in that order!) and then ask to see the person with whom she has an appointment. Now and then, though, you may encounter a visitor who forgoes the formality of introducing himself at the outset, offering only the name of the person he's come to call on:

田中さんをお願いします。

Tanaka-san o onegai shimasu.

I'm here to see Mr. Tanaka.

Office etiquette requires that you ascertain the visitor's name before you announce him; "Mr. Tanaka, some-body's here to see you" would sound distinctly rude in translation (it would hardly pass for courtesy in English). Therefore, you politely inquire:

失礼ですが、どちら様でいらっしゃいますか。

Shitsurei desu ga, dochira-sama de irasshaimasu ka.

I'm sorry, may I have your name, please?

This particular bit of business boilerplate, which can also be used on the telephone to ascertain the identity of a caller, is so well established in the language that it is very often reduced to an abbreviation: the speaker utters only the introductory phrase and leaves the question itself un-spoken.

失礼ですが……

Shitsurei desu ga ...

I'm sorry ...

Having elicited the visitor's name, you need to make sure you've heard it correctly before announcing him. Mispro-nouncing the name of a guest is a hideous lapse of eti-quette, and you should take a moment to confirm the correct pronunciation by repeating it:

渡辺様でございますね。かしこまりました。

Watanabe-sama de gozaimasu ne. Kashikomarimashita.

Mr. Watanabe, of course.

The latter part of this two-sentence formula, the verb *kashikomarimashita* (which, like all Japanese verbs, can constitute a sentence by itself) ought to be memorized right now if you don't know it already. This is the standard way to reply in the affirmative to a guest or visitor. An alternative is the compound verb *shōchi itashimashita*—commit that one to memory right away, too. Either of these expressions, depending on the context, could be variously translated as "Yes, sir," "Certainly, madam," "Of course," "I understand," "Very well," or "I'll do that." To express any of these meanings in conversation with a colleague or peer, you would probably say *wakarimashita*, but not when dealing with a VIP (and visitors are VIPs, at least until they've left).

In cases where the visitor has been expected, a slight variation on the above will serve:

渡辺様でございますね。お待ちいたしておりました。

Watanabe-sama de gozaimasu ne. Omachi itashite orimashita.

Mr. Watanabe, of course. We've been expecting you.

The addition of the latter sentence—*Omachi itashite orimashita* ("We've been expecting you")—will pleasantly reinforce the impression that your outfit really stays on top of individual comings and goings.

Pardon me for asking

失礼ですが……

Shitsurei desu ga ...

Pardon me for asking ...

Anyone accorded the status of a guest—including a visitor to your office—is entitled to special treatment in the Japanese business world. This, no doubt, has much to do with preserving a fundamental distinction between those on the inside (of a business, in this case) and those on the outside, a dichotomy that distinguishes many other facets of Japanese society as well. In recognition of their special status, visitors are to be addressed exclusively in highly polite language, replete with honorific phraseology. Among other things, this means that when you ask a visitor a question, no matter how reasonable or innocent, you must preface your question with an apologetic warning of a potential impertinence, as in the following examples:

失礼ですが、どちら様でいらっしゃいますか。

Shitsurei desu ga, dochira-sama de irasshaimasu ka.

Pardon me for asking, but may I have your name, please?

失礼ですが、どのようなご用件でしょうか。

Shitsurei desu ga, dono yō na goyōken deshō ka.

Pardon me, but may I ask what this is regarding?

失礼ですが、私どもの誰をお訪ねですか。

Shitsurei desu ga, watakushi-domo no dare o otazune desu ka.

I'm sorry, with whom did you wish to speak?

失礼ですが、お約束でございますか。

Shitsurei desu ga, oyakusoku de gozaimasu ka.

I beg your pardon, but do you have an appointment?

Phrasing your questions thus, you can emit a gracious and accommodating glow. The extra touches make all the difference—don't try to simplify things by taking a just-the-facts approach. Leave off the polite disclaimer (*Shitsurei desu ga ...* can be literally translated "This is rude, but ...") and the other bits of polite window dressing, and these same mundane queries sound far less hospitable:

お名前は？

Onamae wa?

Your name?

ご用件は？

Goyōken wa?

What's this about?

うちの誰ですか。

Uchi no dare desu ka.

Who do you want to see?

約束ですか。

Yakusoku desu ka.

Got an appointment?

Obviously, this is the approach to avoid, unless for some reason you want to sound like the churlish turnkey in a prison movie.

Now and then, a visitor may drop in and ask to see someone who's out of the office or in a meeting at the time. Having informed the visitor of the situation and inquired into the nature of the matter at hand (in the manner demonstrated above), you might, depending on your instructions or on the prevailing policy, follow up with:

おさしつかえなければ、代わりの者が承ります が……

Osashitsukae nakereba, kawari no mono ga uketama-warimasu ga ...

If it's not inconvenient, I can inform someone else on the staff that you're here.

You can leave it up to the visitor to decide whether to wait until the person in question is available, talk to someone else instead, or call again another time.

If, on the other hand, policy dictates that anybody without an appointment (including the odd salesperson trying to lodge a foot in the door) be turned away, you need go no further than asking whether your visitor has an appointment. The same polite query introduced above (and the English version as well) has a very different and decidedly chillier ring to it in this context.

失礼ですが、お約束でございますか。

Shitsurei desu ga, oyakusoku de gozaimasu ka.

I beg your pardon, but do you have an appointment?

The follow-up to this is automatic: No appointment, no entry.

Sorry to put you to the trouble of coming

お呼びたていたしまして……

Oyobitate itashimashite ...

Sorry to put you to the trouble of coming.

When you know in advance that someone is coming to see you at the office, it's poor form to keep your visitor waiting after she's arrived—particularly if you're the one who requested the meeting. Still, sometimes it's simply unavoidable, in which case the standard arrangement is for the receptionist (or whoever performs that role) to lead the way to a waiting room or an unoccupied chair, urge the visitor to have a seat, and politely excuse herself, saying something like:

斎藤はただいま参りますので、少々お待ちください。

Saitō wa tadaima mairimasu no de, shōshō omachi kudasai.

If you'd be kind enough to wait just a few moments, Mr. Saito is on his way.

The ensuing brief wait is usually interrupted by the arrival of coffee or tea. Finally, the visitor's host appears, offering a courteous apology:

お待たせいたしました。本日は突然お呼びたて
　いたしまして恐縮です。

Omatase itashimashita. Honjitsu wa totsuzen oyobitate itashimashite kyōshuku desu.

I'm sorry to have kept you waiting. Sorry to put you to the trouble of coming on such short notice today.

Here are some other phrases you might use when greeting a guest, depending on your relationship with the visitor:

お待ちしておりました。どうぞこちらへ。

Omachi shite orimashita. Dōzo kochira e.

We've been expecting you. This way, please.

お久しぶりです。その後いかがですか。

Ohisashiburi desu. Sono go ikaga desu ka.

It's been a long time. How have you been (since we last met)?

先日はいろいろとお世話になりまして……

Senjitsu wa iroiro to osewa ni narimashite ...

Thank you for all your help the other day.

The key phrase *oyobitate itashimashite* ("Sorry to put you to the trouble of coming") conveys consideration for the fact that the speaker has caused his guest some inconvenience and also appreciation for the visitor's forbearance. Granted, the visitor may in fact not have suffered any real inconvenience, and free enterprise itself would soon grind to a halt if people started letting a little inconvenience stand in the way of business. Nevertheless, even if you're about to lodge a complaint or make a demand, politeness requires that you explicitly express your appreciation to any visitor who appears at your request. Here are a couple of alternative phrases, both distinctly formal sounding, that convey essentially the same message:

> わざわざご足労願いまして、申し訳ございません。
>
> *Wazawaza gosokurō negaimashite, mōshiwake gozaima-sen.*
>
> I apologize for putting you to all the trouble of coming here.

> 遠方よりお越しいただきまして、ありがとうございます。
>
> *Enpō yori okoshi itadakimashite, arigatō gozaimasu.*
>
> Thank you for taking the trouble to come all the way over here.

Once these formalities have been dispensed with, the question of sharing a meal might come up, depending on the hour and the nature of the visit:

> お食事はもうおすみですか。
>
> *Oshokuji wa mō osumi desu ka.*
>
> Have you had lunch (or dinner) yet?

In conventional usage, this is not an informational query but an invitation to dine. Etiquette requires that the visitor accept such an invitation, so the only appropriate response is to answer in the negative (with a courteous disregard for the facts, if necessary) and show a willingness to comply. The host, given the power he wields in these situations, may very well have already made the necessary arrangements for a meal. Thus, a warning to the business caller with a timid palate: if you are squeamish at the prospect of dining on the uncooked flesh of anonymous sea creatures and other exotic fare, schedule your visits well before or after the mealtime hours.

We appreciate all that you've done for us

いつもお世話になっております。

Itsumo osewa ni natte orimasu.

We appreciate all that you've done for us.

One of the relatively few Japanese phrases widely recognized outside Japan is *moshi-moshi*, which, among its other functions, is frequently used as a sort of greeting when one answers the telephone. A mere *moshi-moshi* will not suffice, however, when you answer the office phone. Let's say it's ten in the morning and the phone rings at the trading firm Asahi Shōji. You answer:

おはようございます。アサヒ商事です。

Ohayō gozaimasu. Asahi Shōji desu.

Good morning, Asahi Shōji.

or

はい、アサヒ商事でございます。

Hai, Asahi Shōji de gozaimasu.

Hello, Asahi Shōji.

It's essential to promptly state the name of the firm. Of the two alternatives shown above, the first is often preferred, since the initial greeting *ohayō gozaimasu* is thought to strike the sort of cheerful, resonant note that reflects a positive and businesslike atmosphere (not in the afternoon, though). Some firms have rules stating that callers must be greeted with an apology if the phone has rung more than, say, five times:

お待たせいたしました。アサヒ商事でござい
ます。

Omatase itashimashita. Asahi Shōji de gozaimasu.

Asahi Shōji. I'm sorry to keep you waiting.

Generally, the caller's first duty is to identify herself, and that is your cue to say:

いつもお世話になっております。

Itsumo osewa ni natte orimasu.

We appreciate all that you've done for us.

A variation frequently used by speakers of the Kansai dialect prevalent in western Honshu is:

毎度お世話になっております。

Maido osewa ni natte orimasu.

We appreciate all that you've done for us.

To the analytical mind, it may seem inordinately gushy, even by Japanese standards, to use the words *itsumo* (literally, "always") and *maido* ("every time") with every Tom, Dick, and Hiroshi who happens to call. After all, the caller could be anyone, including a corporate extortionist or the disgruntled husband of the boss's mistress. Still, it doesn't pay to be too literal-minded about these things, and none but the most utterly cantankerous caller is likely to object to gratuitous words of appreciation.

Now and then you may encounter a caller who fails to disclose his name at the start of the conversation. In that case, you have to inquire:

失礼ですが、お名前を……
Shitsurei desu ga, onamae o ...
I'm sorry. May I have your name, please?

or

失礼ですが、どちら様でしょうか。
Shitsurei desu ga, dochira-sama deshō ka.
I'm sorry. May I ask who's calling?

As noted elsewhere (see the section entitled "Pardon me for asking") the message to be conveyed is so utterly predictable from the context that the expressions above are very frequently reduced to an abbreviation: the speaker utters only the introductory phrase and leaves the question itself unspoken.

失礼ですが……
Shitsurei desu ga ...
I'm sorry ...

In some cases, such as when the caller has seized control of the conversation and is off and running before you get the chance to ask who's on the other end, it can be more

politic (and more fun) to take a euphemistic approach,
one that has a fairly exact counterpart in English:

> 恐れいります。お名前が聞きとれませんでした
> ので、もう一度お願いいたします。
>
> *Osoreirimasu. Onamae ga kikitoremasen deshita no de,
> mō ichido onegai itashimasu.*
>
> I'm terribly sorry. I'm afraid I didn't quite catch
> your name. Could you say it again, please?

This not only requires the caller to identity himself, but
also subtly reminds him that he should have done so at
the outset.

Let me turn you over to
the person in change of that

担当の者と替わります。

Tantō no mono to kawarimasu.

Let me turn you over to the person in charge of
that.

After you've mastered the job of answering the office
phone in the appropriate businesslike manner (see the
previous section), you still have to make sure the call gets
through to the proper person. When the caller requests to

speak with a specific individual, confirmation is all that's required:

営業二課の森田でございますね。少々お待ちください。

Eigyō ni-ka no Morita de gozaimasu ne. Shōshō omachi kudasai.

Ms. Morita in Business Section Number Two? One moment, please.

or

かしこまりました。営業二課の森田におつなぎいたします。少々お待ちください。

Kashikomarimashita. Eigyō ni-ka no Morita ni otsunagi itashimasu. Shōshō omachi kudasai.

Certainly. I'll connect you with Ms. Morita in Business Section Number Two. One moment, please.

In the event the caller doesn't ask to speak to a specific individual—perhaps she's calling to get information about products or services, for instance—it's up to you to direct the call to the relevant person or department:

ただいま担当の者と替わりますので、少々お待ちください。

Tadaima tantō no mono to kawarimasu no de, shōshō omachi kudasai.

Let me turn you over to the person in charge of that. One moment, please.

or

係の者におつなぎいたしますので、しばらくお待ちください。

___
38

Kakari no mono ni otsunagi itashimasu no de, shiba-raku omachi kudasai.

Just a moment, please. I'll connect you to the person in charge of that.

You are, of course, expected to follow through on the promise conveyed by these words, by making sure the call is directed to whoever is best qualified to answer the caller's questions or otherwise deal with the matter at hand; anything less is passing the buck. You won't endear yourself to anyone by giving people the runaround, no matter how politely or fluently, so it's best to briefly explain what the caller wants and make sure you've found the right person to handle it before transferring the call.

In the event someone calls to lodge a complaint, the first thing to do is to determine whether or not you'll be able to resolve the problem on your own. Sometimes a caller with a complaint simply wants to blow off some steam; with a little patience and tact (and a ready stock of apologetic phrases), you can probably handle that kind of call by yourself. Some complaints, however, call for a response from higher up the line, in which case you *can* pass the buck:

では、責任者に替わりますので、少々お待ちください。

Dewa, sekinin-sha ni kawarimasu no de, shōshō omachi kudasai.

In that case, let me turn you over to my supervisor. Just a moment, please.

I'm afraid we seem to have a bad connection

お電話が遠いようですが……

Odenwa ga tōi yō desu ga ...

I'm afraid we seem to have a bad connection.

Over the past several years, the Japanese business world has become thoroughly infested with mobile telephones. Regardless of whether or not these devices actually increase anyone's efficiency, the frequency with which they are brandished in public suggests that Japan's corporate culture has foregone reticence and polite circumspection in favor of a raucous nonchalance. Like it or not, portable phones are apparently here to stay, so you might as well acquire a few phrases that will help you deal with mobile callers.

The increasing reliance on mobile phones has plenty of built-in drawbacks, one of which stems from the notoriously capricious quality of the connections the phones provide. Signals can break up or fade in and out and background noises often interfere, frustrating all attempts at communication. But even when you're taking a call from someone on a mobile phone and can't make out a word being said, it wouldn't do (and would probably be pointless) to keep asking the caller to repeat everything over and over. At the same time, don't yield to the temptation to simply *pretend* to understand what the caller is saying: merely piping in now and then with a dutiful-sounding *hai* when you actually haven't a clue what the conversation is about would be inviting disaster. Instead, try this:

お電話が遠いようですので、恐れいりますが、
もう少し大きな声でお話しいただけませんか。

Odenwa ga tōi yō desu no de, osoreirimasu ga, mō suko-shi ōki na koe de ohanashi itadakemasen ka.

We seem to have a bad connection. I'm sorry, but could you please speak a little louder?

The direct approach is clearly in the best interests of all concerned. In the event that real communication is still impaired, you could try asking the caller to speak more slowly:

恐れいりますが、もう少しゆっくりとお話しい
ただけませんか。

Osoreirimasu ga, mō sukoshi yukkuri to ohanashi itadake-masen ka.

I'm sorry, but could you please speak a little more slowly?

If it's obvious that no amount of speaking up or slowing down will make the caller intelligible under the present circumstances, state the case in plain terms, lay out the options, and end the conversation.

申し訳ございません。お電話がまだ遠いようで
すが……間違いがありますと大変ですので、
後ほどおかけ直しいただけますか。それとも、
こちらからおかけいたしましょうか。

Mōshiwake gozaimasen. Odenwa ga mada tōi yō desu ga ... Machigai ga arimasu to taihen desu no de, nochi-

*hodo okakenaoshi itadakemasu ka. Sore tomo, kochira
kara okake itashimashō ka.*

I'm terribly sorry. We still seem to have a bad connection. I'm afraid we may get our signals crossed,
so either let me call you back or please call me
back.

The ubiquity of mobile phones and their well-known
quirks have inevitably encouraged the more devious-
minded to invent imaginary phone troubles as a pretext
for dodging conversations they'd rather not have. Anyone
so inclined, however, should be forewarned: unless you
are a highly skillful liar, some false note in your voice will
probably give away the ruse. You might succeed in avoid-
ing the caller, but you could also be forfeiting his trust in
the future.

She's away from her desk at the moment

ただいま席をはずしております。

Tadaima seki o hazushite orimasu.

She's away from her desk at the moment.

Let's say you answer the phone and the caller asks to
speak with Ms. Mori, one of your colleagues:

森さんをお願いいたします。

Mori-san o onegai itashimasu.

I'd like to speak to Ms. Mori, please.

Ms. Mori, however, is nowhere in sight, although she apparently hasn't gone out because her sweater is still draped over the back of her chair. You can say:

ただいま席をはずしております。

Tadaima seki o hazushite orimasu.

She's away from her desk at the moment.

The implication is that, although momentarily unavailable, she's around somewhere and therefore can be reached or will be able to return the call fairly soon. This is *not* the phrase to use when taking a call for a colleague who's away from the office—if the caller tries again ten minutes later and is then informed that the person he's looking for is out for the afternoon, he's liable to think he was deliberately misled the first time. Therefore, when someone is out of the office, say so, and tell the caller what time she'll be back, if you can:

ただいま外出しておりますが、4時には戻ってまいります。

Tadaima gaishutsu shite orimasu ga, yoji ni wa modotte mairimasu.

She's out of the office at the moment. She'll be back at four o'clock.

Then ask to take a message:

戻りましたら、折り返しお電話さしあげましょうか。

Modorimashitara, orikaeshi odenwa sashiagemashō ka.

Shall I have her call you when she gets back?

or

おさしつかえなければ、ご伝言承ります。

Osashitsukae nakereba, godengon uketamawarimasu.

I'll be happy to take a message, if you like.

The use of the phrase *osashitsukae nakereba* (literally, "provided it wouldn't cause you any inconvenience") in the second example above emphasizes that there is no obligation to leave a message—it's entirely up to the caller. Incidentally, it's not a good idea to inquire into the reason for the call. Even if you're only asking out of a desire to be helpful, the question is apt to strike the caller as presumptuous.

Certain telephone situations call for particular delicacy and tact. Suppose, for instance, someone calls the office around ten o'clock in the morning and asks to speak to a colleague of yours named Sato who's ordinarily expected to be in by nine-thirty. If you say he's not in yet, the caller might conclude that Sato's habitually tardy and undependable, so instead you should say:

佐藤は本日、立ち寄りがありまして11時ごろに
参ります。

Satō wa honjitsu, tachiyori ga arimashite jūichi-ji goro ni mairimasu.

Mr. Sato had to make a stop on the way in today.
He'll be here around eleven.

Similarly, if Mr. Tamura, the boss, has taken the day off to play golf with a client, you needn't burden anyone calling with the details. Just say:

田村は本日、出張で留守にしておりますが、明日は出社いたします。

Tamura wa honjitsu, shutchō de rusu ni shite orimasu ga, myōnichi wa shussha itashimasu.

Mr. Tamura is away on business today, but he'll be back tomorrow.

Note the absence of the honorific *-san* in the last two examples. Business etiquette requires that, when talking to someone outside the business, you refer to people who work for the same firm you do—even the boss—by name only.

I'm sorry for calling out of the blue like this

お電話で失礼とは存じますが……

Odenwa de shitsurei to wa zonjimasu ga ...

I'm sorry for calling out of the blue like this.

Someday you'll probably have to request a service from someone you've never dealt with before. In principle, making such a request requires a face-to-face meeting; even in these phone-crazed times, the Japanese business world still attaches mystical importance to the need for an in-the-flesh encounter to seal the start of any business project or relationship. Nevertheless, it's often more practical to make the initial overture over the telephone. Therefore, as a way of acknowledging the notion that people are supposed to meet before they discuss business—and scolding yourself for not being there in person—you have to be apologetic about it when you want to sound out someone over the phone prior to making a formal business request. There's a ready-made phrase for this purpose:

お電話で失礼とは存じますが……

Odenwa de shitsurei to wa zonjimasu ga ...

It's really not proper for me to be doing this over the phone, but ...

Having made the obligatory bow to convention, you can proceed to sketch out your tentative proposal. Here are a couple of alternative phrases that will enable you to broach the subject at hand somewhat more directly:

突然のお願いで恐縮ですが……

Totsuzen no onegai de kyōshuku desu ga ...

I apologize for springing this on you so unceremoniously, but ...

折り入ってお願いがございまして……

Ori-itte onegai ga gozaimashite ...

There's something I'd really like to ask of you.

Once you've actually met the other person (and you certainly must, if you're going to be doing business together), subsequent conversations will flow more naturally and it will be easier to make further requests, eliminating the need for this sort of language. To pique the other person's interest in getting together to talk, it seldom hurts to appeal to self-interest:

詳細はお目にかかった折にお話しいたしますが、
けっしてご損になるお話ではございません。

Shōsai wa ome ni kakatta ori ni ohanashi itashimasu ga, kesshite goson ni naru ohanashi de wa gozaimasen.

I'll be glad to give you all the details when we meet. You certainly won't be sorry when you've heard what I have to say.

A somewhat different but equally standard usage of the first phrase of this section applies to telephone exchanges in which the caller is introducing himself. Let's say you've just taken over a new sales position and are calling customers to let them know the torch has been passed to you. You might start out this way:

お電話で失礼とは存じますが、このたび御社の
担当となりましたブラウンと申します。

Odenwa de shitsurei to wa zonjimasu ga, kono tabi on-sha no tantō to narimashita Buraun to mōshimasu.

It's really not proper for me to be doing this over the phone, but let me introduce myself. My name's Brown. I'll be in charge of your account from now on.

This, of course, represents only a cursory introduction. You still have to call on each customer and formally introduce yourself in person, at the earliest possible opportunity.

I'm sorry to be calling so late

夜分遅く恐れいります。

Yabun osoku osoreirimasu.

I'm sorry to be calling so late.

Nobody likes getting a call from the office after hours when they're trying to relax. Considering the amount of time people spend working, it goes without saying that, if at all possible, their nightly respite ought not to be disturbed. Sometimes it can't be helped, though. Emergencies arise and may occasionally require you to get hold of a colleague or a superior who's already left for the day. In such a case, the standard greeting is, naturally, apologetic:

夜分遅く恐れいります。

Yabun osoku osoreirimasu.

I'm sorry to be calling so late.

or

夜分に恐れいります。

Yabun ni osoreirimasu.

I'm sorry to be calling so late.

The first word of each phrase above, *yabun*, literally means "evening" or "nighttime," so this wouldn't be the greeting to use on a Saturday afternoon. Generally speaking, *yabun* covers the period from about eight in the evening until morning. At other times, you can use a different greeting, such as:

おくつろぎのところを恐れいります。

Okutsurogi no tokoro o osoreirimasu.

I'm sorry to be intruding on your private time.

Let's put the proper greeting into the context of the phone conversation you are reluctantly going to initiate. Suppose you find yourself forced to call your boss (Mr. Yano, the *kachō*, or head of your section) at home. You dial the number and his wife or daughter answers, and you say:

夜分遅く恐れいりますが、矢野課長はご在宅で
しょうか。私、部下のブラウンと申します。

Yabun osoku osoreirimasu ga, Yano-kachō wa gozaitaku deshō ka. Watakushi, buka no Buraun to mōshimasu.

I'm sorry to be calling so late. Is Mr. Yano available? This is Mr. Brown, one of his employees.

Presuming the boss is indeed at home, his wife can identify the caller to him by name and put him on. Now you greet him:

こんな時間にお呼び立ていたしまして申し訳ご
ざいません。実は……

Konna jikan ni oyobitate itashimashite mōshiwake goza-imasen. Jitsu wa ...

I'm terribly sorry to be calling you at this hour. The situation is this ...

After providing a concise summary of the situation and receiving your instructions, don't neglect to apologize again as you sign off:

夜分お騒がせいたしました。

Yabun osawagase itashimashita.

I'm sorry to have interrupted your evening.

Due to unavoidable circumstances

よんどころない事情で……

Yondokoro-nai jijō de ...

Due to unavoidable circumstances ...

Naturally, it's best to establish and scrupulously maintain a reputation as someone who knows how to keep a promise. Still, now and then you'll probably be forced to cancel an appointment for reasons that are beyond your control and that wouldn't bear explaining. The phrase *yondokoro-nai jijō* ("unavoidable circumstances") offers uniform coverage for this sort of situation, as in:

申し訳ありません。よんどころない事情で、明日伺えなくなりました。

Mōshiwake arimasen. Yondokoro-nai jijō de, myōnichi ukagaenaku narimashita.

I'm very sorry, but due to unavoidable circumstances I'm afraid I won't be able to make it tomorrow.

In principle, this sort of reference to *yondokoro-nai jijō* is supposed to elicit the other party's implicit understanding. After all, unavoidable circumstances can interfere with anyone's plans. Sooner or later, everyone has to fall back on this excuse, so it has a sort of universal validity, like a free pass—which will be summarily revoked if you start using it too often.

An alternative to the *yondokoro-nai jijō* approach is to attribute the situation to unspecified difficulties:

申し訳ありません。ちょっと問題が生じまして
明日伺えなくなりました。

Mōshiwake arimasen. Chotto mondai ga shōjimashite myōnichi ukagaenaku narimashita.

I'm very sorry, but a small problem has come up and I'm afraid won't be able to make it tomorrow.

This is not always the wisest approach to take because the mention of *mondai* ("problem"; the same goes for *toraburu*, "trouble") is likely to pique the other party's curiosity. You may be stuck if you're asked what sort of trouble it is, and the other party may well feel entitled to ask, since you brought the subject up.

Just as "unavoidable circumstances" constitute a permissible reason for canceling or postponing an appointment, "a previous engagement" is almost always an acceptable reason for turning down an invitation. When you're invited by a colleague or a superior to go out for drinks after work and don't want to go, for instance, you needn't hurt anyone's feeling by being evasive or unduly blunt. Just say:

あいにく先約がございまして……

Ainiku senyaku ga gozaimashite ...

I'm afraid I have a previous engagement.

The standing "previous engagement" is a familiar dodge, of course, being universally available, but for all anyone knows you might actually have one. While the other person is essentially compelled to accept your excuse, it's polite to acknowledge the courtesy of the invitation. One effective way to do so is to request a rain check:

次の機会にはよろしくお願いいたします。

Tsugi no kikai ni wa yoroshiku onegai itashimasu.

Let's do it another time.

I'm afraid I have to ask your indulgence

お聞き苦しい点もあるかと存じますが……

Okikigurushii ten mo aru ka to zonjimasu ga ...

I'm afraid I'll have to ask your indulgence ...

It's considered good form to strike a note of humility when you first address a meeting or a gathering of some sort. Call it a variation on the "aw shucks, folks" approach: you play up your own inadequacy as a preventive measure to keep listeners from expecting too much. The tone is apologetic:

風邪をひいておりまして、お聞き苦しい点もある
るかと存じますが、ご容赦ください。

Kaze o hiite orimashite, okikigurushii ten mo aru ka to
zonjimasu ga, goyōsha kudasai.

I've got a bit of a cold, and I'm afraid I'll have to
ask your indulgence. I hope you'll pardon me.

or

わたくしは技術系の人間で、このような場でお
話しするのは初めてでございます。お聞き苦
しい点もあるかと存じますが……

Watakushi wa gijutsu-kei no ningen de, kono yō na ba
de ohanashi suru no wa hajimete de gozaimasu. Okiki-
gurushii ten mo aru ka to zonjimasu ga ...

I've always worked on the technical end of things,
and this is the first time I've ever spoken at a
gathering like this. I'm afraid I'll have to ask
your indulgence.

The implication is that the speaker might be forgiven if
the speech is less than riveting. These words are merely a
polite formality, of course, and the speaker who utters
them may go on to deliver an address that is the very
model of wit and eloquence.

The following is an assortment of other standard lines
to have on hand when you're addressing a meeting.

When handing out copies to provide listeners with relevant information:

ご判断の材料になればと存じまして……

Gohandan no zairyō ni nareba to zonjimashite ...

I thought perhaps this data might be worth considering.

When you're about to launch into a technical explanation:

専門用語で恐縮ですが……

Senmon-yōgo de kyōshuku desu ga ...

I'm afraid you'll have to bear with some technical
   terminology.

When you intend to present verbally only an outline of
the matter at hand (having provided the listeners with a
more detailed explanation on paper):

詳細はお手元のレポートをご覧ください。

Shōsai wa otemoto no repōto o goran kudasai.

Please refer to the report in front of you for the details.

When you want to call the listeners' attention to a particular point in order to prevent any misunderstanding:

それからついでに申しますと……

Sore kara tsuide ni mōshimasu to ...

While I'm at it, let me just say ...

When you're wrapping up your remarks:

以上、説明の至らない点も多々あったかと存じ
   ますが、ご清聴ありがとうございました。

*Ijō, setsumei no itaranai ten mo tata atta ka to zonji-
   masu ga, goseichō arigatō gozaimashita.*

That's about it. I'm afraid there may be many relevant points that I've neglected to address, but I
   thank you for your kind attention.

We did absolutely everything we could, but

できるだけのことはしたんですが……

Dekiru dake no koto wa shita n' desu ga ...

We did absolutely everything we could, but ...

Sometimes, in spite of your very best efforts, you just can't deliver the goods. You do have to deliver the bad news, though, and let the customer or the boss know that the situation has not yielded the hoped-for results. Don't fail to note that you gave it your best shot, using either the phrase above or the following one:

八方手を尽くしましたが……

Happō te o tsukushimashita ga ...

We exhausted every possibility, but ...

The standard explanations (or excuses) for failure to meet expectations tend to cite severe time pressures or material obstacles, such as budgetary constraints, as in the following examples:

できるだけのことはしたんですが、なにぶんコ
ストの問題がありまして……

Dekiru dake no koto wa shita n' desu ga, nanibun ko-suto no mondai ga arimashite ...

We did absolutely everything we could, but after all, we kept running into cost problems.

八方手を尽くしましたが、なにぶん急なことだ
ったものですから。

*Happō te o tsukushimashita ga, nanibun kyū na koto
datta mono desu kara.*

We exhausted every possibility, but after all, it was
a rush job.

In business, of course, results are everything. In the absence of results, excuses are as common as weeds, and there's no guarantee that yours will get a sympathetic hearing. If you are unfairly taken to task, you're entitled to defend yourself, but don't harp on the fact that you did your best—you've said so already, and you don't want to overemphasize that your best wasn't good enough. Instead, wait for an appropriate opening and say:

せめて事情だけでも聞いてください。

Semete jijō dake de mo kiite kudasai.

At least let me explain the circumstances.

Then calmly review the process that led to the disappointing outcome, relate the current situation, and indicate what can be done to improve things, in that order. Keep in mind that the ability to confront setbacks without losing one's head is the mark of a professional.

I'm afraid
you've put your finger on it

痛いところを衝かれました。

Itai tokoro o tsukaremashita.

I'm afraid you've put your finger on it.

It's time again to make your periodic report to the customer regarding the project you're working on for her. After you've provided a brief outline of the situation, you give her a chance to comment or ask questions, and she proceeds to zero directly in on the weakest part of your program—the part you glossed over, hoping it would pass unnoticed. Ouch! Now you can say:

痛いところを衝かれました。

Itai tokoro o tsukaremashita.

I'm afraid you've put your finger on it.

You could also say:

まさにそこが問題点でありまして……

Masa ni soko ga mondai-ten de arimashite ...

That's just where the problem lies.

Or you could try to leaven the atmosphere with a little base flattery:

さすがは高山さん、鋭いご指摘です。

57

Sasuga wa Takayama-san, surudoi goshiteki desu.

It takes a keen eye like yours, Ms. Takayama, to see the situation so clearly.

When you're already aware of flaws or other points in your presentation that are likely to be addressed, it makes sense to be sure you're ready to answer for them. Nevertheless, it doesn't pay to be glib—you might inadvertently convey a tell-me-something-I-don't-already-know sort of impudence, which would only work against you. Make sure you clearly acknowledge the other party's wisdom in being meticulous about the details—don't let them leave thinking you might have let things slide if the problem hadn't been pointed out. Take charge:

痛いところを衝かれました。まさにそこがこの
企画の問題点でありまして、これについては
次のように私どもは考えております。

Itai tokoro o tsukaremashita. Masa ni soko ga kono ki-kaku no mondai-ten de arimashite, kore ni tsuite wa tsugi no yō ni watakushi-domo wa kangaete orimasu.

I'm afraid you've put your finger on it. That's just where the problem lies, and here's what we're thinking of doing about it.

This way, the client is credited with pointing out the problem, so it's out in the open, and now you're taking steps to deal with it. Everyone's happy, more or less.

Could you spare me a little of your time?

ちょっとお時間をいただけますか。

Chotto ojikan o itadakemasu ka.

Could you spare me a little of your time?

When the time comes to relay information to or consult with one of the higher-ups at the office, you can't just thrust yourself into the other person's path as if you were asking directions from a passerby on the street. You have to obliquely inquire whether the circumstances would permit you a hearing:

ちょっとお時間をいただけますか。

Chotto ojikan o itadakemasu ka.

Could you spare me a little of your time?

The basic query *ojikan o itadakemasu ka* ("May I have some of your time?") constitutes an invaluable piece of business phraseology and can be adapted to serve a variety of functions and occasions. Here are two examples.

When you want to request a meeting with someone outside the firm:

ぜひお目にかかってお話ししたいのですが、お時間をいただけますか。

Zehi ome ni kakatte ohanashi shitai no desu ga, ojikan o itadakemasu ka.

I'd really like to get together and talk things over with you. Could you spare me a little of your time?

When concluding a visit to someone at another firm:

貴重なお時間をいただきましてありがとうございました。

Kichō na ojikan o itadakimashite arigatō gozaimashita.

Thank you very much for letting me have some of your precious time.

The same words, *ojikan o itadakemasu ka*, can also be used to convey an entirely different meaning. In this case the request is for *more* time, as in:

この件は即答いたしかねますので、お時間をいただけますか。

Kono ken wa sokutō itashikanemasu no de, ojikan o itadakemasu ka.

That's something that really can't be settled right on the spot. Could you give me a little time to look into it?

The longer it takes to respond, of course, the longer the matter is left dangling, and the more likely you are to get a call from the other party pressing you for an answer. You, in turn, could try hauling out that key phrase once again:

もう少しお時間をいただけますか。

Mō sukoshi ojikan o itadakemasu ka.

Could I have a little more time?

Now, however, these words may carry the sound of someone dragging his feet.

I'm sorry
to put you to the trouble

お手数をおかけします。
Otesū o okake shimasu.
I'm sorry to put you to the trouble

Over the course of an ordinary working day, it's likely
you will need to request a service or helping hand from
one of your colleagues any number of times—this, among
other reasons, is why people work together in offices. At
these times it's essential to present your request in an ap-
propriately polite manner. People can get very touchy
about unscheduled requests, even simple ones delivered
in the line of duty, unless the proper overtures are made.
For the sake of continuing good relations, due consideration must be given to the other person's point of view.
Then again, there's no call to grovel on the office floor
every time you need a fax sent or a file delivered, either.
Simply recite these magic words:

お手数をおかけします。
Otesū o okake shimasu.
I'm sorry to put you to the trouble.

This simple phrase can work wonders. You would do well to memorize it now and use it often—when approaching one of the higher-ups for advice on dealing with a problem, for example, or when on the phone asking someone in another department to look something up for you.

A similar expression, and one you'll probably hear all the time around the office, is *osoreirimasu*, which could be variously translated as "pardon me for asking" or "if you please," or sometimes as "thank you." This phrase, like *otesū o okake shimasu*, often functions as a courteous formality attached to a question or request, as in:

恐れいりますが、その戸を締めてもらえますか。

Osoreirimasu ga, sono to o shimete moraemasu ka.

Would you mind closing that door, please?

The difference between these two expressions is worth noting. The latter, *osoreirimasu*, has a more perfunctory ring to it; it tends to come across as an obligatory formality. Moreover, *osoreirimasu*, as a statement of the speaker's feelings, represents an approach to the situation emphasizing one's own point of view. As noted above, it's essential to convey a concern for the other person's point of view, in light of the effort she's being asked to exert, and that is exactly the function that *otesū o okake shimasu* performs. Given this basic distinction between these two phrases, it's important to use the right one at the right time. Let's say you're winding up a visit to another firm and one of the employees there has put together some materials for you to take along when you leave. In this case, you may not have had to make any request, but you can leave a good impression by showing courteous appreciation for the service you've received:

お手数をおかけしました。

Otesū o okake shimashita.

I'm sorry to have put you to the trouble.

Whatever it takes

そこをなんとか……

Soko o nantoka ...

Whatever it takes ...

In the event you find yourself prevailing on a reluctant colleague to do a crucial and difficult favor, or in a situation where a customer or a supplier is balking at an important request, you may have to resort to abject begging. You might as well do it right:

> そこをなんとか……けっして軽く考えているわ
> けではございませんので。
>
> *Soko o nantoka ... Kesshite karuku kangaete iru wake de*
> *wa gozaimasen no de ...*
>
> Whatever it takes, please. Believe me, this is no
> laughing matter.

or

> そうおっしゃらず、そこをなんとか……
> *Sō ossharazu, soko o nantoka ...*

Please don't say that. Look, whatever you can do ...

No matter how many times you're refused, keep coming back, and pour on the pathos. You want to convey the impression that you're tottering at the edge of a mighty precipice (think of Mount Fuji) and the other person is your last and only hope of survival. Focus on the objective, have no shame, and you can win: for a good many people, a truly pathetic appeal for help is hard to refuse.

This strategy can be combined with other elements to yield a number of possible approaches:

The promise-of-reciprocation approach:

> 埋め合わせは必ずいたします。ですから今回だ
> けは、ひとつ……
>
> *Umeawase wa kanarazu itashimasu. Desu kara konkai dake wa, hitotsu ...*
>
> I promise I'll return the favor. So just this once, please, whatever it takes ...

The soon-to-be-homeless approach:

> ご承諾いただけませんと、わたくし、社に帰れ
> ませんので……
>
> *Goshōdaku itadakemasen to, watakushi, sha ni kaeremasen no de ...*
>
> If I can't get your okay on this, I won't be able to show my face at the office anymore.

The have-pity-on-the-little-guy approach, especially useful for someone from a small firm addressing someone (here a Mr. Kato) from a big corporation:

> 加藤さんのお力でなんとかしていただけると、

今日まで信じてまいりました。加藤さんなら
きっとご理解いただけると……

Katō-san no ochikara de nantoka shite itadakeru to,
konnichi made shinjite mairimashita. Katō-san nara
kitto gorikai itadakeru to ...

Up to now I've believed that somehow you'd come
through for us, Mr. Kato. I was sure that you
were the one who would understand ...

Obviously, the idea is to emphasize and appeal to the
other person's good side, implying that it would be un-
worthy of him—downright sinful—to turn you down.

Whenever
it's convenient for you

ご都合にあわせます。
Gotsugō ni awasemasu.
Whenever it's convenient for you.

It's an established principle of business etiquette—when
requesting a meeting or fixing the date for a meeting
you've requested—that the other person's schedule takes
precedence over other considerations. At such times, one
of these phrases may come in handy:

ご都合のよい日をご指定ください。

Gotsugō no yoi hi o goshitei kudasai.

Just name a day that would be convenient for you.

わたくしどもは、中村様のご都合にあわせます。

Watakushi-domo wa, Nakamura-sama no gotsugō ni awa-semasu.

We can accommodate your schedule, Mr. Nakamura.

お手すきのお時間がございましたら……

Otesuki no ojikan ga gozaimashitara ...

If there should be some particularly convenient
time for you ...

Another approach is to politely propose a date yourself:

もし、おさしつかえなければ、4月21日ではい
かがでしょうか。

*Moshi, osashitsukae nakereba, shigatsu nijūichi-nichi de
wa ikaga deshō ka.*

If it wouldn't be too inconvenient, how would
April 21 be?

The elaborately polite examples above convey a self-effacing
attitude. The following one has a slightly more casual ring:

ご都合がよろしければ、4月21日、あるいは4月
23日ではいかがでしょうか。

*Gotsugō ga yoroshikereba, shigatsu nijūichi-nichi, aruiwa
shigatsu nijūsan-nichi de wa ikaga deshō ka.*

If you could fit it in, would either the 21st or the
23nd of April be all right?

On occasion, the task of arranging a meeting with someone might entail prevailing on a third party to introduce

you or help smooth the way. If you actually need some-one to act as an intermediary, the phrase to use is:

よろしくお取りなしください。

Yoroshiku otorinashi kudasai.

Please intercede for me.

If you simply want to meet someone, presuming you know the third party well enough to ask the favor, you could say:

よろしくお引き合わせください。

Yoroshiku ohikiawase kudasai.

Please introduce me.

The expression *ohikiawase* ("introduce or bring together") is not to be confused with *ohikimawashi*, which probably sounds similar. The latter is used to make a different sort of request:

よろしくお引き回しをお願いします。

Yoroshiku ohikimawashi o onegai shimasu.

I hope you don't mind if I look to you for guid-ance.

This is the kind of thing a new employee might say to a more experienced colleague or upon being introduced to the person in charge of the account at a client firm.

Sorry to spring this on you, but

突然で悪いんだけど……

Totsuzen de warui n' da kedo ...

Sorry to spring this on you, but ...

The privileges of seniority are reflected in the types of expressions favored by bosses and older employees when they address their subordinates and younger colleagues. When making a request, the higher-ups tend to dispense with elaborate phraseology and rituals of formal courtesy, simply because they're allowed to, unlike the rest of us. For instance, as noted elsewhere, the phrase *osoreirimasu ga* is a standard polite preface for impromptu requests made by ordinary mortals, but you won't hear that one from the boss. You're far more likely to hear one of these phrases:

突然で悪いんだけど……

Totsuzen de warui n' da kedo ...

Sorry to spring this on you, but ...

忙しいところを悪いんだけど……

Isogashii tokoro o warui n' da kedo ...

Sorry to interrupt you, but ...

突然で申し訳ないが……

Totsuzen de mōshiwake nai ga ...

Sorry to be asking on such short notice, but ...

Any of these would generally be followed by a routine request, as in:

突然で悪いんだけど、この数字をちょっとチェックしてくれる？

Totsuzen de warui n' da kedo, kono sūji o chotto chekku shite kureru?

Sorry to spring this on you, but could you check these figures for me?

忙しいところを悪いんだけど、ちょっとこれをコピーしてくれない？

Isogashii tokoro o warui n' da kedo, chotto kore o kopī shite kurenai?

Sorry to interrupt you, but could you make me a copy of this?

突然で申し訳ないが、今日は1時間ほど残業してほしいんだ。

Totsuzen de mōshiwake nai ga, kyō wa ichiji-kan hodo zangyō shite hoshii n' da.

Sorry to be asking on such short notice, but I need you to put in an hour or so of overtime today.

This is not to suggest that people with seniority are entirely exempt from the rules of etiquette. The introductory phrases above do convey a sense of courtesy, though not the self-humbling version of courtesy one usually encounters. Seniority be damned, it would be considered rude of any boss to make a sudden request without the such a preface attached. Gone are the days when an office staff would put up some gruff old codger hollering *Oi, ocha* ("Hey, tea here!") at the female employees. Some senior types actually make an effort to sound sympathetic when asking their subordinates to do things for them:

面倒なことを頼むが、ひとつやってくれないか。

Mendō na koto o tanomu ga, hitotsu yatte kurenai ka.

I know it's a pain, but would you take care of it for me?

君でないとわからないことだから。

Kimi de nai to wakaranai koto da kara.

See, you're the only one who can handle this.

After having given the order and the employee has acknowledged it, he might say:

ご苦労だね。

Gokurō da ne.

It's a tough job (and I appreciate your doing it).

Sometimes a boss or a senior colleague will couch a request in euphemistic phraseology. A prominent example is the expression *tsuide no toki* ("when you have time"), as in:

ついでのときでいいんだが、これを頼む。

Tsuide no toki de ii n' da ga, kore o tanomu.

When you have time, take care of this for me.

It wouldn't be a good idea to take these words literally. However courteous they sound, the conventional implication is that the speaker wants you to drop whatever you're doing and carry out the request.

However poor my efforts
may be

及ばずながら……

Oyobazunagara ...

However poor my efforts may be ...

People are subjected to all sorts of requests and demands in the business world, some bigger than others. When you have been asked to take on some particularly important task or a major job, you may need to express your willingness to do so in a formal and self-deprecating manner. The same applies if you're given an important new assignment or a promotion. On all these occasions, modesty first:

> 及ばずながら、ご期待にそえますよう尽力いた
> します。
>
> *Oyobazunagara, gokitai ni soemasu yō jinryoku itashimasu.*
>
> However poor my efforts may be, I'll try to live up to your expectations.

or

> 微力ながらお役に立ちたいと存じます。
>
> *Biryoku nagara oyaku ni tachitai to zonjimasu.*
>
> Meager as my talents may be, I'll be glad to help out.

If you really want to get humble about it, you could trot out one of these:

至らない点もあるかと存じますが、全力を尽くす所存です。

Itaranai ten mo aru ka to zonjimasu ga, zenryoku o tsukusu shozon desu.

I'm afraid I may not be equal to the job in some respects, but I intend to give my all.

or

行き届かぬところもあるかと思いますが、私のようなものでよろしければお力に……

Yukitodokanu tokoro mo aru ka to omoimasu ga, watashi no yō na mono de yoroshikereba ochikara ni ...

If you're sure that, with all my shortcomings, I'm the person for the job, then I'll do my best.

Hokey as they may sound, the examples above are for use in formal situations. Nobody talks that way under normal circumstances. To convey your enthusiastic consent in a more casual situation, you could use any of the following:

私でよければ、喜んで……

Watashi de yokereba, yorokonde ...

If I'm really the one you want, I'll be glad to.

お安いご用ですよ。

Oyasui goyō desu yo.

No trouble at all.

そういうことでしたら、ぜひお任せください。

Sō iu koto deshitara, zehi omakase kudasai.
If that's all it is, by all means, leave it to me.

いつでもおっしゃってください。
Itsudemo osshatte kudasai.
Certainly, anytime at all.

Bear with me this time

勘弁してください。
Kanben shite kudasai.
Bear with me this time.

Imagine you're faced with a regular customer who's pressing you to quote him a lower price, despite the fact that you've already met him more than halfway. You've conceded most of your profit margin and yet the customer adamantly and unreasonably continues to insist that you go lower still. He won't give up, but you can't possibly give another inch, and there's nothing to be done about it. That's the moment to heave a desperate, audible sigh and plead for mercy:

勘弁してください。
Kanben shite kudasai.
Bear with me this time.

Nobody likes to take no for an answer, and it's especially hard to refuse a regular client, even when the request is clearly unreasonable. Poorly handled, a refusal can easily cause resentment and much worse—it might end up costing you the account. Therefore, no matter how painful it is to contain your indignation, it's imperative that you refrain from even a hint of criticism of, or displeasure at, the customer's bare-knuckled tactics. To the absolute bitter end, play it humbly:

私どもといたしましては、これが精一杯のところでございまして……

Watakushi-domo to itashimashite wa, kore ga sei-ippai no tokoro de gozaimashite ...

From our point of view, this is really as far we can possibly go.

掛け値なしでこれだけでございます。

Kake-ne nashi de kore dake de gozaimasu.

It's no more than an honest price, nothing added.

どうか事情をお察しください。

Dōka jijō o osasshi kudasai.

Please, try and understand our situation.

If, despite your most stoic forbearance and gentle words, you're still unable to come to reasonable terms with this most persistent customer, there's one more trick left in the bag—play for time:

では一両日お時間をいただけないでしょうか。

Dewa ichiryōjitsu ojikan o itadakenai deshō ka.

Well then, could you possibly give me a day or two?

Your request implies that you'll try to find a way to give him what he wants, but you can actually use the time to consult your superiors and try to find some other way out. Besides, if you give the other guy a little time to cool off, he might realize he's been out of line and come around to your way of thinking.

It's a matter of company policy

社の方針ですので……

Sha no hōshin desu no de ...

It's a matter of company policy.

It's not particularly difficult to turn down a request when you're on equal footing with the other party or dealing from a position of relative strength. You certainly wouldn't want to sound high and mighty about it, of course, but if you choose the right expression you can effectively get the message across, either directly or indirectly, without giving undue offense. Suppose, for instance, someone is trying to put the squeeze on you for special treatment or an unreasonable discount. You can decline without ruffling anyone's feathers by saying:

社の方針ですので、どうかご容赦ください。

Sha no hōshin desu no de, dōka goyōsha kudasai.

I'm afraid we simply can't—it's a matter of company policy.

Let's say you're being hounded by one of those high-pressure sales people—don't mince words:

> あいにくですが、今回は見送らせていただきます。
>
> *Ainiku desu ga, konkai wa miokurasete itadakimasu.*
>
> Sorry, but I'll pass this time.

or

> せっかくですが、今回は見送らせていただきます。
>
> *Sekkaku desu ga, konkai wa miokurasete itadakimasu.*
>
> Sorry you've gone to all the trouble, but we'll pass this time.

If you'd rather offer an excuse than just say no, try this one:

> すでにほかの業者さんと約束しておりまして……
>
> *Sude ni hoka no gyōsha-san to yakusoku shite orimashite ...*
>
> I'm afraid we've already made arrangements with another dealer.

Or you can simply toss out this all-purpose wet blanket:

> ちょっとむずかしいですね。
>
> *Chotto muzukashii desu ne.*
>
> That would be difficult.

If it seems more appropriate to take an indirect approach, you can clearly communicate your refusal without ever having to state it in so many words. Conventional usage favors this indirect strategy—drop a few hints and let the person getting the bad news fill in the rest. There are plenty of expressions available that are well suited to it.

Here's a small sampling:

けっこうなお話とは思いますが……
Kekkō na ohanashi to wa omoimasu ga ...
What you've told me is all very interesting, but ...

お役に立ちたいのはやまやまですが……
Oyaku ni tachitai no wa yamayama desu ga ...
I certainly wish I could help you, but ...

いろいろお骨折りいただきましたが……
Iroiro ohone-ori itadakimashita ga ...
It's been kind of you to go to all this trouble, but ...

当方には身にあまるお申し出でございますが……
Tōho ni wa mi ni amaru omōshide de gozaimasu ga ...
Your offer is more than generous, but ...

ご事情はお察ししますが……
Gojijō wa osasshi shimasu ga ...
I understand your situation, but ...

Is that an order?

それは業務命令ですか。
Sore wa gyōmu-meirei desu ka.

Is that an order?

If a person seeks employment in the business world and accepts the status of employee, it goes without saying that she's expected take direction from and execute the commands of her superiors in the workplace. But what about those times when a boss wants something done that just isn't part of the job? How do you say no?

Consider this scenario: the head of the section you work in is someone who takes particular delight in going out with the gang for drinks after work, while you yourself aren't nearly as keen on that sort of thing, having long since endured enough karaoke for one lifetime. One day the boss announces:

金曜日に課の親睦会をやりたいから、みんな出席してくれ。

Kin'yōbi ni ka no shinboku-kai o yaritai kara, minna shusseki shite kure.

I'd like to have a little section get-together on Friday, and I want you all to come.

It so happens you have something else planned for Friday night. If you have to go out drinking with the people in your section, you'll have to cancel your other plans. That would be more than even you could bear, so you fire back with:

課長、それは業務命令ですか。

Kachō, sore wa gyōmu-meirei desu ka.

Is that an order, boss?

There, now you've shown him, now he knows who's the boss on Friday night. He certainly can't order you to give up your precious free time, so there's nothing he can say. On the other hand, no matter how good a time you have on Friday night, Monday morning will come around eventually, and you know who'll be the boss then. Maybe you spoke out a bit too quickly—maybe you should have thought this through more carefully.

As a peremptory comeback to a boss who acts as if the employees exist to serve his every whim, *sore wa gyōmu-meirei desu ka* could be an effective shot across the bow, but it's also the kind of hardball remark that tends to engender ill will. If you're prepared to live with the consequences, fine; if not, you'd better take a different tack.

Let's go back to the original scenario. This time, after the boss announces his plans to monopolize everyone's Friday night, you make your apologies and fish up a polite (possibly fictional) excuse, such as:

あいにく金曜日は先約がございます。

Ainiku kin'yōbi wa sen'yaku ga gozaimasu.

I'm afraid I have a previous commitment on Friday.

このところ体調をくずしております。

Kono tokoro taichō o kuzushite orimasu.

I have to take it easy for health reasons.

日本語の教室があり、今週は私がスピーチをすることになっております。

Nihongo no kyōshitsu ga ari, konshū wa watashi ga supīchi o suru koto ni natte orimasu.

I've got Japanese class and I have to make a speech this week.

Nobody's going to dispute the validity of your excuse,

provided you don't make it too imaginative. This way, you can keep your plans and still maintain cordial relations at the office. Just make sure that you don't run into the gang while you're out painting the town on your own Friday night.

On my own authority

私の一存では……

Watakushi no ichizon de wa ...

On my own authority ...

A knack for quick thinking is always an asset, but when a client asks you a question and you don't know the answer, it wouldn't be smart to just improvise. In the same way, it wouldn't be wise if, in the midst of an important negotiation, you took it upon yourself to single-handedly make decisions you had no authority to make. As an employee, you represent the firm, and in your business dealings with people outside the firm your words are generally taken to represent the official company position—there's no going back later to explain that you were only speaking for yourself. That's why, when presented with a question you can't answer or a decision that exceeds your authority, the best policy for the time being is to refrain from taking a position, saying:

私の一存ではお答えいたしかねますので、少し
お時間をいただけますか。

*Watakushi no ichizon de wa okotae itashikanemasu no
de, sukoshi ojikan o itadakemasu ka.*

I'm afraid I really can't answer that on my own
authority. Can you give me a little time?

This is far preferable to pretending to be able to answer
the question and making some equivocal statement to
disguise the fact that you're in over your head, which can
lead to endless disputes later on over what you did or
didn't say.

A couple of alternative expressions that perform the same
function are:

あいにくその件は、私にはわかりかねます。

Ainiku sono ken wa, watakushi ni wa wakarikanemasu.

I'm afraid that's something that I myself don't know
enough about.

申し訳ありません。担当の者でないとお答えで
きません。

*Mōshiwake arimasen. Tantō no mono de nai to okotae
dekimasen.*

I'm very sorry, but that's a question only the person in charge can answer.

Of course, if you left it at that you'd sound indifferent
and distinctly unhelpful, so it's best to follow up with
something that shows you intend to render satisfaction,
such as:

ただ今、係の者に問い合わせてまいります。

Tadaima, kakari no mono ni toiawasete mairimasu.

Let me go and ask the person in charge.

or

上の者と相談いたしまして、あらためてご返事
いたします。

*Ue no mono to sōdan itashimashite, aratamete gohenji
itashimasu.*

I'll be glad to give you an answer once I've had a
chance to consult with my superiors.

I'll take it into consideration

検討いたします。

Kentō itashimasu.

I'll take it into consideration.

You can't always be expected to know what to do when
someone makes you a business proposal or presents you
with a suggestion or piece of advice. You may want to
think it over; very often that's the wisest course. The expression to use is:

検討いたします。

Kentō itashimasu.

I'll take it into consideration.

There are a couple of variations on this basic phrase that

shouldn't be confused with one another. The first variation is fairly straightforward, conveying the idea that the speaker intends to closely examine the pros and cons of the matter without delay:

さっそく検討いたします。

Sassoku kentō itashimasu.

I'll take it into immediate consideration.

The second, grammatically tortuous variation (which nevertheless conveys the same literal meaning as the basic phrase *kentō itashimasu*) tends to be employed as a euphemism for polite refusal.

検討させていただきます。

Kentō sasete itadakimasu.

I'll take it into consideration.

With these words, the speaker is often implying that he probably won't be giving the matter much further consideration. It may well be that he's already dismissed what he's just been told, having heard the other person out just for the sake of politeness or curiosity; knowing that it would be rude to flatly reject the idea on the spot, he's simply holding his tongue. This is the way business people often deal with unwelcome requests, and it's also a well-known strategy for responding to well-intentioned advice that, under the circumstances, can't be followed.

Whichever version of the phrase you use, the effect is to leave the listener in the dark for the time being. If it's a request that's been presented, these words don't clearly let the other person know whether to hold out hope or give up and look elsewhere. For that reason, politeness requires you to convey your answer in unequivocal terms at the very next opportunity that presents itself, either in person or over the phone. Start out this way:

> ご依頼の件は検討いたしましたが……
> *Goirai no ken wa kentō itashimashita ga ...*
> I've considered your request carefully ...

or

> ご助言の件は検討いたしましたが……
> *Gojogen no ken wa kentō itashimashita ga ...*
> I've considered your advice carefully ...

or

> ご提案の件は検討いたしましたが……
> *Goteian no ken wa kentō itashimashita ga ...*
> I've considered your proposal carefully ...

If the answer is no, say so without further delay, and don't forget to add a courteous apology:

> ご依頼の件は検討いたしましたが、今回は見送
> らせていただきます。まことに残念ですが、
> ご容赦くださいますようお願いいたします。
>
> *Goirai no ken wa kentō itashimashita ga, konkai wa miokurasete itadakimasu. Makoto ni zannen desu ga, goyōsha kudasaimasu yō onegai itashimasu.*
>
> I've considered your request carefully, but I'm afraid I'll have to pass this time. I'm sorry to disappoint you, and I hope you understand.

You'll be expected to provide a reason for your refusal, so be prepared to explain.

Let's just wait
and see what happens

少し様子を見てみましょう。

Sukoshi yōsu o mite mimashō.

Let's just wait and see what happens.

For some people, at least, the notion of a business executive is associated with decisiveness. Be that as it may, the Japanese business world is home to plenty of so-called executives whose employees have to pressure them into making decisions. Often enough, the response to such pressure may take the form of one of these phrases:

少し様子を見てみましょう。

Sukoshi yōsu o mite mimashō.

Let's just wait and see what happens.

ちょっとペンディングにしておこう。

Chotto pendingu ni shite okō.

Let's leave the matter pending for a while.

事態の推移を今しばらく見守って……

Jitai no suii o ima shibaraku mimamotte ...

Let's wait and see how the situation develops.

The latter expression is most famously associated with do-nothing politicians, but it's definitely heard in business circles as well. The attitude it reflects is thought by some to represent the wisdom of the seasoned veteran, who treads slowly and lightly where fools rush in. After all, the thinking goes, the vagaries of business—fluctuating interest rates and exchange rates, wily maneuvers by one's rivals—are impossible to foresee; the future, good or bad, is impenetrable to even the sharpest eye. Therefore, they say, in a situation where you can't decide which course to follow the safest thing is to stay where you are. Based on this type of reasoning, it's not necessarily true that those who keep falling back on the *sukoshi yōsu o mite miyō* approach are lazy, indecisive, or dull-witted; in their own world, they're the enlightened ones.

With all due respect

お言葉ではございますが……
Okotoba de wa gozaimasu ga ...
With all due respect ...

Harmony is bliss, but there are times when a person just can't agree with what's been said and feels compelled to voice an opposing view. As a preface to the statement of a contrary position, depending on the situation, this phrase might serve:

お言葉ではございますが……
Okotoba de wa gozaimasu ga ...

With all due respect ...

This is not an expression to toss around indiscriminately, however. For some people, it has a harsh ring; it's probably not the words themselves—the language is both formal and, well, respectful—but the fact that they signal opposition. It would seem the Japanese business world in general is painfully unaccustomed to people disagreeing with each other out loud, however respectfully. The use of this phrase can convey the impression that no effort is being made to soften the shock of contradiction and may even suggest that the speaker is willing to risk a falling out. Obviously, this is not one to use on cherished customers and other regular associates. It's probably best reserved for use in in-house discussions and brainstorming sessions, occasions when it's acceptable to let fly with all sorts of opinions and ideas.

There may come a day when want you try out a phrase like this on your boss when taking issue with some dubious instructions on a particular business matter. Do so with utmost care. You're playing with fire to begin with, so don't make matters worse by interrupting him in mid-sentence with a fiery *okotoba de wa gozaimasu ga*—that would almost certainly push him over the edge. Instead, let him exhaust his argument thoroughly, and when you're sure he's finished (or at least ready to take a breather), start out with one of these:

差し出がましいようですが……
Sashide-gamashii yō desu ga ...
I know this might sound a bit forward of me, but ...

お言葉を返すようで心苦しいのですが……
Okotoba o kaesu yō de kokorogurushii no desu ga ...

I would hate to sound presumptuous for saying this, but ...

けっしてお言葉を返すわけではありませんが……

Kesshite okotoba o kaesu wake de wa arimasen ga ...

I certainly don't intend any disrespect by this, but ...

With one of these phrases, you're still in the safety zone. Probably the only time when you could get away with saying *okotoba de wa gozaimasu ga* to your boss would be when defending yourself against an unfair accusation or a harsh criticism that's based on a misunderstanding of the facts. Otherwise, steer clear.

I certainly appreciate what you're saying

おっしゃることはよくわかります。

Ossharu koto wa yoku wakarimasu.

I certainly appreciate what you're saying.

Even if a client or customer has taken an utterly unreasonable position, you have to state your opposition in a way that minimizes the possibility of exacerbating the situation. One way of doing this is to start out by clearly acknowledging the other person's point of view:

おっしゃることはよくわかります。

Ossharu koto wa yoku wakarimasu.

I certainly appreciate what you're saying.

お気持ちはよくわかります。

Okimochi wa yoku wakarimasu.

I definitely understand how you feel.

たしかにその通りだと存じます。

Tashika ni sono tōri da to zonjimasu.

Without a doubt, it's just as you've said.

なるほどお客様のおっしゃることはごもっとも
です。

*Naruhodo okyaku-sama no ossharu koto wa gomottomo
desu.*

The situation is indeed just exactly as you've de-
scribed it.

Whether or not you actually consider the other party's
viewpoint valid is an entirely different matter, of course,
and one best kept private. The idea is to open with an in-
gratiating stroke aimed at putting the listener in a mood
to entertain a different point of view. Pulling off a grace-
ful transition into the latter is the second part of this one-
two approach:

おっしゃることはよくわかります。ただ私ども
といたしましては……

*Ossharu koto wa yoku wakarimasu. Tada, watakushi-
domo to itashimashite wa ...*

I certainly appreciate what you're saying. It's just

that, speaking from our point of view ...

お気持ちはよくわかります。たしかにそういう
　見方もございますが……

*Okimochi wa yoku wakarimasu. Tashika ni sō iu mika-
ta mo gozaimasu ga ...*

I definitely understand how you feel. That's certainly one valid way to look at the situation, but ...

たしかにその通りだと存じます。ただ、こうい
　う見方もあるのではないでしょうか。

*Tashika ni sono tōri da to zonjimasu. Tada, kō iu mikata
mo aru no de wa nai deshō ka.*

Without a doubt, it's just as you've said. Only, I
wonder whether it might not also be possible to
look at it this way: ...

なるほどお客様のおっしゃることはごもっとも
　です。しかし、このようにさせていただけばも
　っとご満足いただけるのではないでしょうか。

*Naruhodo okyaku-sama no ossharu koto wa gomottomo
desu. Shikashi, kono yō ni sasete itadakeba motto gomanzoku itadakeru no de wa nai deshō ka.*

The situation is indeed just exactly as you've de-
scribed it. And yet, it seems to me perhaps you
might be even happier in the end if we were to
handle it this way: ...

If there's a hint of flattery in your approach, all the better
to prepare the way for your own position, the essence of
which is to make what's already good even better. The
thing to remember is, you can avoid giving needless offense by withholding your own views until you've first

paid the obligatory tribute to the other person's ideas. Then, when you finally get around to your opinion, you can more or less casually mention your doubts or dissent. Here's one more example:

お話を伺って大変勉強になりました。基本的に
は賛成ですが、二三、感じたことをお話しし
てよろしいでしょうか。

Ohanashi o ukagatte taihen benkyō ni narimashita. Kihon-teki ni wa sansei desu ga, ni-san, kanjita koto o ohana-shi shite yoroshii deshō ka.

What you've said is very enlightening. Basically, I agree with you, but there are just a couple of things I'd like to talk over, if I might.

I wonder
if I might ask a question?

ひとつ質問してもよろしいですか。
Hitotsu shitsumon shite mo yoroshii desu ka.
I wonder if I might ask a question?

Due to a pervasive aversion to spontaneity that character-izes most official venues of communication in the Japanese business world, in-house meetings can resemble liturgical pageants in their solemn predictability. Let's suppose, how-ever, that you work for a firm where some meetings include actual give-and-take. Let's say you're at such a meeting and you happen to disagree with a point just made by someone else in attendance. Before you state your own view (the correct view, needless to say), the rules say you must first seek and be granted permission to speak. One of these phrases will serve:

ひとつ質問してもよろしいですか。

Hitotsu shitsumon shite mo yoroshii desu ka.

I wonder if I might ask a question?

ちょっとよろしいですか。

Chotto yoroshii desu ka.

Excuse me, may I say something?

二三、確認させていただきたいのですが……

Ni-san, kakunin sasete itadakitai no desu ga ...

There are a couple of things perhaps you could clear up for me.

Beyond enabling you to take the floor, an expression such as one of these performs two functions: it directs the focus of the discussion toward the points you're going to challenge and also signals that you're about to take issue with something that's already been said. You can continue by directing attention back to the remarks you disagree with, and then—only then—weigh in on the other side. Suppose, for instance, you're going to challenge some dubious statement made by a colleague named Murata. You could say:

ただいま村田さんは＿＿＿＿とおっしゃいました
　　が、私は反対の立場です。

Tadaima Murata-san wa _____ to osshaimashita ga, watashi wa hantai no tachiba desu.

Just now Mr. Murata said _____, but I take the opposite view.

or

ただいま村田さんは_____とご指摘なさいましたが、私は反対の立場です。

Tadaima Murata-san wa _____ to goshiteki nasai-mashita ga, watashi wa hantai no tachiba desu.

We've just heard Mr. Murata make the point that _____, but I take the opposite view.

or

ただいまの村田さんのご意見には、問題点がひとつあります。

Tadaima no Murata-san no goiken ni wa, mondai-ten ga hitotsu arimasu.

There's one problem with the position just stated by Mr. Murata.

In those cases when the in-house meeting is not an occasion for elaborate rituals of politeness, you needn't be equivocal about contradicting someone, though you must always be at least as circumspect as you would in English. Be clear when stating your own position and explain your reasons in the simplest and most direct terms possible. Above all, make sure you have a firm and accurate grasp of the views you're speaking up against, to avoid the embarrassment of working yourself into a lather over something you only half-understood.

There's one little thing that bothers me

ちょっと気になったんだが……

Chotto ki ni natta n' da ga ...

There's one little thing that bothers me, though.

Advice and instructions from a boss to an employee tend to be conveyed in language far less formal than that used when a message is going in the opposite direction. A section head looking over a report submitted by one of the people under him might use one of these phrases:

ちょっと気になったんだが……

Chotto ki ni natta n' da ga ...

There's one little thing that bothers me, though.

欲を言えば……

Yoku o ieba ...

What I would really to see is ...

These expressions serve as gentle lead-ins to a request for further exertions. The speaker is implying that, while not quite up to standard yet, the employee's work merits approval in some respects, or at least this is an acknowledgment of the efforts made so far. It would do little for the employee's morale, after all, to summarily dismiss the fruits of her hard work as unacceptable. A lighter touch can take some of the sting out of having her efforts found wanting, as in:

> ちょっと気になったんだが、この経費はもう少し削る必要がありそうだね。
>
> *Chotto ki ni natta n' da ga, kono keihi wa mō sukoshi kezuru hitsuyō ga arisō da ne.*
>
> There's one little thing that bothers me, though. These expenses need to be reduced just a bit more.

> いいね、よくやってくれた。ただ欲を言えば、ここのところはこうしたほうが……
>
> *Ii ne, yoku yatte kureta. Tada yoku o ieba, koko no tokoro wa kō shita hō ga ...*
>
> Ah, very good, you've done a nice job. But what would really make this great is to take this part here ...

The second example above demonstrates the two-step method: first show some appreciation for the employee's efforts thus far, then indicate the areas that remain in need of attention. Given this kind of gentle handling, the employee can be expected to accept the boss's new instructions without any hard feelings.

On occasion, however, the kid glove treatment may not be warranted. It's an unlucky employee who submits a report for review and hears this:

> もっといいやり方はないものかな。
>
> *Motto ii yarikata wa nai mono ka na.*
>
> There must be a better way of doing this.

These words indicate that the work is seriously deficient—bad enough for the boss to skip the customary words of encouragement and reach for the sledge hammer. In this case the employee's whole approach may have to be revised. Still, even that probably wouldn't be as bad as being shouldered aside while the boss steps in and takes over the job himself, saying something like:

よし、あとはおれがやる。

Yoshi, ato wa ore ga yaru.

Okay, I'll take over from here.

Make sure to check it

ちゃんとチェックしといて。

Chanto chekku shitoite.

Make sure to check it.

There are all sorts of everyday Japanese expressions that incorporate words and fragmented bits of words that were once English, and the business world in particular is rife with this sort of hybrid phraseology. If the existence of such expressions represents a bridge between the two languages, it must be a suspension bridge: once across, the grammatical roles, distinctive pronunciation, and varieties of meaning that give a word its identity in English all tend to be suspended. Whatever's left is reinterpreted under the dominion of Japanese-language patterns and conventions and generally emerges all but unrecognizable to English speakers who knew that word back home before it left Kansas.

Nevertheless, there are a few English-derived terms that retain at least some of the flavor of their origins. Consider some of the various uses of the familiar phrase *chekku suru*, from the English verb "check":

この契約書をチェックするようにたのまれた。

Kono keiyaku-sho o chekku suru yō ni tanomareta.

I've been asked to check over this contract.

日の丸社の動きをチェックしてくれ。

Hinomaru-sha no ugoki o chekku shite kure.

Check and see what Hinomaru (a rival firm) is up to, will you?

スケジュールをチェックしといて。

Sukejūru o chekku shitoite.

Check your schedule, would you?

In the first example, *chekku suru* means something like "look over (something) to make sure it's okay." In the second, it means "investigate or look into." In the third example, the meaning is "consult," and here both the Japanese sentence and the translation are identically ambiguous: depending on the context, the message conveyed could be either "consult your schedule to confirm a standing appointment" or "consult your schedule to see if a given period of time is open." Here's one more example demonstrating the broad range of usage that applies to *chekku suru*:

おれ、秘書の川村さんをチェックしてるんだ。

Ore, hisho no Kawamura-san o chekku shite 'ru n' da.

I've been checking out that secretary, Ms. Kawa-
mura.

Japanese business talk is full of phrases featuring "English" borrowings, due in part to the pseudo-cosmopolitan
cachet attached to such terminology in some circles.
What follows is only a meager sampling:

コールバックしてくれる？

Kōru-bakku shite kureru?

Would you call me back?

アポを取っといて。

Apo o tottoite.

Set up an appointment.

リアクションを見といてくれ。

Riakushon o mitoite kure.

Keep an eye out and watch their reaction.

エクスキューズを考えといて。

Ekusukyūzu o kangaetoite.

Think up an excuse.

オフレコにしといて。

Ofu-reko ni shitoite.

Let's keep this off the record (confidential).

Put your heart into it

気を入れてやってくれ。

Ki o irete yatte kure.

Put your heart into it.

The section chief has just unveiled an important new project and now, to give it a proper launching, he wants to whip up the troops into a frenzy of exertion. His impassioned appeal for best efforts all around finds expression in one of the following phrases:

ここはひとつ、気を入れてやってくれ。

Koko wa hitotsu, ki o irete yatte kure.

All right now, let's see you really put your heart into it.

ここはひとつ、本腰を入れてやってくれ。

Koko wa hitotsu, hongoshi o irete yatte kure.

All right now, I want you to really give it all you've got.

Next, one of the employees who's caught the spirit (or who wants to curry favor with the boss) takes up the cry:

よし、みんな気合を入れていこうぜ。

Yoshi, minna kiai o irete ikō ze.

All right, guys, let's fire up!

or

そうだ、気を引き締めていこう。

Sō da, ki o hikishimete ikō.

Yeah, let's get tough!

Soon the whole section is ablaze with fiery zeal, every last woman and man pledged to make the new project a brilliant success—another triumph for enlightened phraseology.

The basic phrase *ki o ireru* ("to put one's heart into it" or "do something in earnest") is also frequently employed to exhort an employee who's judged to be neglecting his work or not taking it seriously enough. The boss might say:

どうしたんだ。もっと気を入れてやらないとだめじゃないか。

Dō shita n' da. Motto ki o irete yaranai to dame ja nai ka.

What's the matter with you? You'd better get serious about what you're doing.

At the heart of all the key phrases in this section is *ki* ("spirit"). While *ki o ireru* and *ki o hikishimeru* ("to get tough or brace oneself for action") represent positive things you can do with your *ki*, there are negative things as well. Here are three:

気をちらす

ki o chirasu

to be distracted or unable to concentrate

気をとられる

ki o torareru

to lose one's focus or be distracted

気を抜く
ki o nuku
to lose one's drive or zest

The latter phrase might be used by the boss, once again chewing someone out for making a careless mistake:

気を抜いているから、こういう単純なミスをするんだ。しっかりしろ。

Ki o nuite iru kara, kō iu tanjun na misu o suru n' da. Shikkari shiro.

You're losing your edge—that's why you let an easy one like this get by you. Snap out of it!

You, of all people

ブラウン君ともあろうものが……
Buraun-kun to mo arō mono ga ...
You, of all people, Brown.

Now and then, even the most conscientious of us is apt to slip up. When your turn comes around it may come as a shock, since your overall track record is doubtless exemplary. In any case it probably won't escape the notice of your boss, who will certainly bring the matter to your attention:

ブラウン君ともあろうものが、こんなミスをす
るとは信じられん。いったいどうしたんだ。

*Buraun-kun to mo arō mono ga, konna misu o suru to
wa shinjiraren. Ittai dō shita n' da.*

I can hardly believe that you, of all people, Brown,
dropped the ball like this. What in god's name is
going on?

Lucky for you you're not the section chief. When he
comes in for a scolding from his superior, the weight of
his responsibilities will probably be used to grind his face
in it, as in:

君、課長ともあろうものがそんな弱気なことで
どうする。いやしくも管理者なら……

*Kimi, kachō to mo arō mono ga sonna yowaki na koto
de dō suru. Iyashiku mo kanri-sha nara ...*

You, the section head, of all people, how can you
be such a lightweight? If you were any kind of a
manager at all ...

Both of the examples above convey two messages at once:
the boss is both delivering a reprimand for blundering
or carelessness and at the same time expressing disappointment that the employee has failed to measure up to
expectations. The latter message may be intended as a
backhanded form of positive motivation, implying that
the employee is being held to a higher standard due to
her superior abilities or the importance of her position.
On the other hand, these words could also have a nasty,
sarcastic edge, suggesting that this one screw-up has con-
firmed long-held doubts and proven that the employee's
abilities had obviously been overrated. In this sense, a
simple reprimand like this can have far more impact than

half an hour of ranting and raving—particularly when the target is someone with otherwise strong credentials and, up to now, a presumably bright future.

The tactic of emphasizing the unexpectedness of seeing a job botched underlies the frequent usage of these expressions as well:

君らしくもない。

Kimi-rashiku mo nai.

This just isn't like you.

まさか君が、こんなミスをしでかすとは夢にも思わなかったよ。

Masaka kimi ga, konna misu o shidekasu to wa yume ni mo omowanakatta yo.

It never occurred to me that you would have messed things up like this, not even in my wildest dreams.

A judicious boss might also sound a note of consolation by appealing directly to the employee's pride:

君の実力はこの程度じゃないはず。

Kimi no jitsuryoku wa kono teido ja nai hazu.

I ought to be able to expect more from someone of your abilities.

If you keep this up

こんなことがつづくようなら……
Konna koto ga tsuzuku yō nara ...
If you keep this up ...

There's a whole armory of sharp-edged phrases—some lethal, some not—available to a boss taking an employee to task for bungling his duties. One of the more menacing of these is frequently wielded thus:

こんなことがつづくようなら、私にも考えがある。
Konna koto ga tsuzuku yō nara, watashi ni mo kangae ga aru.
If you keep this up, I'll be forced to do something about it.

If you hear these words, alarm bells should ring within. Your livelihood could be in jeopardy; if not, perhaps a demotion is being contemplated, possibly a downgrade to some meaningless and woebegone sinecure—the dreaded desk by the window. At the very least, the prospect of a resoundingly negative personnel evaluation may be in the offing.

If whatever mistake you've made provokes this kind of rebuke, it must have been a serious transgression. A trivial slip-up would ordinarily meet with a more tolerant response, such as:

今回は初めてだから仕方がないが……

Konkai wa hajimete da kara shikata ga nai ga ...

Well, you're new at this, and that can't be helped.

Serious blunders fall into another category, however, and are dealt with far more severely. Watch out if you hear something like this:

> 君はいつもこんないいかげんなことをやっているのか。
>
> *Kimi wa itsumo konna iikagen na koto o yatte iru no ka.*
>
> Is this your normal way of doing things—screwing up like this?

This type of comment (it's not really a question) strongly suggests that the speaker has lost faith in you. Even worse would be to hear something like this:

> ほかの人にもそんな態度をとっているのか。
>
> *Hoka no hito ni mo sonna taido o totte iru no ka.*
>
> Is this the way you act around everyone?

Now you've got the boss feeling sorry for himself—he only tolerates you because he's such a patient and understanding guy (right!), and look how you've repaid his kindness. You'd better try and win back his trust while you still can, because from here it's not too far downhill to the direst expressions of outright dismissal:

> やる気がないんだったら辞めてもらってもいいんだぞ。
>
> *Yaru ki ga nai n' dattara yamete moratte mo ii n' da zo.*
>
> If you don't feel like doing your job, you can always quit, you know.

首を洗って待ってるんだな。

Kubi o aratte matte 'ru n' da na.

Prepare for the worst. You'll be hearing about this.

もう会社に来るな。

Mō kaisha ni kuru na.

Don't bother coming into work anymore.

Saying your sorry won't cut it

すみませんですむと思うか。

Sumimasen de sumu to omou ka.

Saying you're sorry won't cut it.

Beating up on the hired help may be thought by some to be just one more part of the job of being a boss, but it takes a certain level of discernment to be effective at it. A supervisor can't afford to coddle an employee he happens to be fond of or is grooming for an important post in the future, or she'll never learn how demanding the job really is. At the same time, if he's overly critical the employee is apt to lose confidence or grow resentful at the harsh medicine she's being made to take for her own good. The question of just how heavy or light a touch to use when bringing someone into line is a perplexing one for which there are no ready-made answers.

Two frequently heard and thoroughly typical expressions of reprimand are:

すみませんですむと思うか。

Sumimasen de sumu to omou ka.

Saying you're sorry won't cut it.

and

いったい何を考えているんだ。

Ittai nani o kangaete iru n' da.

What the hell's the matter with you?

The first of these emphasizes the seriousness of a mistake that affects business—unlike a social or personal lapse, it can't be erased with a mere apology. The second example, for which a more literal translation might be "What in the world are you thinking of?" isn't really a question but a blunt admonition to shake off all distractions and earnestly concentrate on the task at hand. This is the kind of phrase that's often delivered in the heat of the moment, when people tend to fall back on cliches.

When the reading of the riot act is directed at a veteran employee, it might include one of the following:

何年この仕事をやってるんだ。

Nannen kono shigoto o yatte 'ru n' da.

How many years have you been here (at this job)?

いつまでも新人のつもりでいるんじゃない。

Itsu made mo shinjin no tsumori de iru n' ja nai.

You can't keep making these rookie mistakes forever.

The first example is a purely rhetorical question. It implies that, given the extent of his experience, the employee ought to know better, and this is expected to get him to show greater discretion in the future. While it may sound demeaning, the second expression is supposed to accomplish the same thing.

There's no excuse for what I've done

返す言葉もございません。

Kaesu kotoba mo gozaimasen.

There's no excuse for what I've done.

When a client confronts you with a serious mistake you've made or presents a justifiable grievance or criticism, the only thing for it is to acknowledge that you were wrong, wholeheartedly and without qualification. There are any number of ways to do this, such as:

返す言葉もございません。

Kaesu kotoba mo gozaimasen.

There's no excuse for what I've done.

一言もありません。

Ichigon mo arimasen.

There's absolutely nothing I can say (in my own defense).

お説の通りです。
Osetsu no tōri desu.
You're entirely correct.

いちいちごもっともです。
Ichi-ichi gomottomo desu.
Every single thing you've said is perfectly true.

おっしゃる通りでございます。
Ossharu tōri de gozaimasu.
I'm afraid it's exactly as you've said.

Forget about trying to explain, abandon all those pathetic excuses, and just beg forgiveness:

面目ありません。
Menboku arimasen.
I'm ashamed of myself.

面目次第もございません
Menboku-shidai mo gozaimasen.
I'm truly ashamed.

This is not a moment for levity, but if you know the other person well enough, you can perhaps afford to use a less lugubrious expression than those above. For instance:

穴があったら入りたい気持ちです。
Ana ga attara hairitai kimochi desu.
If I had a hole I'd crawl into it.

The standard pattern in these cases is: humbly accept the blame, express your most sincere regrets and have your apologies accepted, and then solemnly vow that the mistake will never be repeated. The following would be one way to handle the lot:

> このたびの不始末につきましては、返す言葉も
> ございませんが、以後二度とこのようなこと
> のないよう注意いたします。どうかご容赦く
> ださい。
>
> *Kono tabi no fu-shimatsu ni tsukimashite wa, kaesu kotoba mo gozaimasen ga, igo nido to kono yō na koto no nai yō chūi itashimasu. Dōka goyōsha kudasai.*
>
> There's no excuse for the carelessness that's been shown, but we'll certainly take steps to ensure that this sort of thing never happens again. Please forgive us.

This approach would be used when dealing with a lapse that's considered to be the fault of the company as a whole. If the blame clearly lies with one unfortunate individual, it calls for a more personal statement, such as:

> 私の不注意（私の不勉強）で大変ご迷惑をおか
> けしました。以後気をつけますので、どうか
> お許しください。
>
> *Watakushi no fu-chūi (Watakushi no fu-benkyō) de taihen gomeiwaku o okake shimashita. Igo ki o tsukemasu no de, dōka oyurushi kudasai.*
>
> I'm afraid I've created serious trouble for you as a result of my carelessness (inattention). I hope you can forgive me. I'll be more careful in the future.

Our mistake

私どもの手違いで……

Watakushi-domo no techigai de ...

Our mistake ...

Mistakes don't just happen—people make them. If the customer got the wrong goods or was quoted the wrong price, or if the shipment didn't arrive on the date it was supposed to, it's because somebody wasn't doing his job properly. That requires an apology, which might go like this:

> 私どもの手違いで、大変ご迷惑をおかけしました。
>
> *Watakushi-domo no techigai de, taihen gomeiwaku o okake shimashita.*
>
> It was an error on our part, and we regret causing you this inconvenience.

> 私どもの手違いで、とんだ粗相をいたしました。
>
> *Watakushi-domo no techigai de, tonda sosō o itashimashita.*
>
> This was inexcusable carelessness, and it was our mistake.

> 私どもの手違いで、お客様がご注文なさった品の入荷が一日遅れてしまいました。ご迷惑をおかけしまして申し訳ございません。

Watakushi-domo no techigai de, okyaku-sama ga gochū-
mon nasatta shina no nyūka ga ichinichi okurete shi-
maimashita. Gomeiwaku o okake shimashite mōshiwake
gozaimasen.

Mistakes made by this office caused a one-day delay
in the arrival of your order. I apologize for this
unfortunate disruption.

The key phrase *watakushi-domo no techigai* ("our mistake")
amounts to an acceptance of responsibility for what's
gone wrong. In its place, a similar phrase can be used instead:

手違いがございまして……

Techigai ga gozaimashite ...

There's been an error.

Here the assumption of responsibility is conspicuously
absent, as in "mistakes were made." It may be that it's un-
clear which side actually made the mistake, but even so,
when an apology leads off with this phrase, the effect
tends to be that of a statement made for form's sake
rather than a statement of sincere regret.

Sometimes the blame can be attributed to a particular
individual, such as the person in charge of the account.
In that case, this phrase will come in handy:

係の者の手違いで……

Kakari no mono no techigai de ...

Due to an error by the person in charge ...

All too often it's left up to someone other than the guilty
party to make the proper apologies. If you get stuck with
this sorry duty, you may point out that you yourself are

not responsible for the mistake, but the important thing is to convey the regrets of the firm itself, which must assume ultimate responsibility. For example:

係の者の手違いで、ご指摘のように請求金額に
間違いがございました。さっそく訂正しまし
てお送りいたします。ご迷惑をおかけしました。

Kakari no mono no techigai de, goshiteki no yō ni seikyū-kingaku ni machigai ga gozaimashita. Sassoku teisei shimashite ookuri itashimasu. Gomeiwaku o okake shimashita.

Due to an error by the person in charge, the amount you were billed was incorrect, as you indicated. I'll prepare a correct invoice and send it to you right away. I apologize for the inconvenience this has caused you.

In apologizing for a mistake made by someone working under you, one of these lines might also serve:

ご注意いただかなければ気がつかないところで
した。さっそく係に申して改めさせます。

Gochūi itadakanakereba ki ga tsukanai tokoro deshita. Sassoku kakari ni mōshite aratamesasemasu.

If you hadn't pointed it out we would never have known. I'll tell the person who's handling this immediately and have him straighten it out right away.

不行き届きで申し訳ございません。以後このよ
うなことがないよう、厳重に申し伝えます。

Fu-yukitodoki de mōshiwake gozaimasen. Igo kono yō na koto ga nai yō, genjū ni mōshitsutaemasu.

113

I apologize for this carelessness. I'll set my people straight and make sure this never happens again.

I'll go back to square one

一から出直します。
Ichi kara denaoshimasu.
I'll go back to square one.

It takes guts to admit that your whole approach needs a complete overhaul. Then again, it's far better to admit it yourself than have someone else point it out. Sometimes the best way to get back on track after a foul-up is to return to the basic principles and think things through once more. Demonstrating a renewed determination to do well is also an effective way to show contrition for a lapse. These phrases are used for that purpose:

一から出直します。
Ichi kara denaoshimasu.
I'll go back to square one.

一からやり直します。
Ichi kara yarinaoshimasu.
I'll start over from scratch.

Once a person gets used to a job, he almost inevitably starts to lose the intensity and heightened sense of purpose that he felt as a newcomer. An experienced hand can become overly confident of his own abilities as, perhaps unconsciously, he learns to choose the easy way whenever possible and avoid anything that promises to be difficult. This is a trap that many people fall into, and there are any number of reasons to break out of it—above all, the discovery that it's led you to make a serious mistake. If that happens you may have to plead your case before the boss, and you'll have to show that you're prepared to re-vamp your whole program. This way, for example:

もう一度チャンスをください。一からやり直し
　　ます。

Mō ichido chansu o kudasai. Ichi kara yarinaoshimasu.

Please let me have another chance. I'll start over
　　from scratch.

It might be too late, of course. The head office may already be sending in your replacement and issuing orders for your exile to the boondocks. Even if that's the case, you may be able redeem yourself somewhat in the eyes of your boss and colleagues by humbly and stoically embracing your fate with words such as these:

わかりました。一から出直します。

Wakarimashita. Ichi kara denaoshimasu.

I understand. I'm going back to square one.

or

わかりました。雑巾がけからやり直します。

Wakarimashita. Zōkin-gake kara yarinaoshimasu.

I understand. I'll start over from the very bottom.

As you know

ご承知のように……

Goshōchi no yō ni ...

As you know ...

When you address a meeting, it's a good idea to review the facts and circumstances in the background before launching into your own views on the matter at hand. You can start out by reviewing the points on which everyone is expected to be united, and you can employ one of these introductory phrases to make it clear that's what you're doing:

ご承知のように……

Goshōchi no yō ni ...

As you know ...

ご案内のように……

Goannai no yō ni ...

As you are no doubt aware ...

ご存じの通り……

Gozonji no tōri ...

As you are aware ...

Unless you lead off with an expression of this sort, your listeners probably won't know if what you're saying is supposed to be common knowledge or your own individual interpretation of things. Using one of these phrases not only enables you to clearly stake out the common ground at the outset but will also lend a sense of organization to your remarks. Virtually any topic can be introduced this way:

ご承知のように、今期の営業実績は……

Goshōchi no yō ni, konki no eigyō jisseki wa ...

As you know, our sales for this quarter are ...

ご案内のように、このたびの役員改選は……

Goannai no yō ni, kono tabi no yakuin kaisen wa ...

As you are no doubt aware, the recent board of directors' election was ...

ご存じの通り、このプロジェクトの基本的なコンセプトは……

Gozonji no tōri, kono purojekuto no kihon-teki na konseputo wa ...

As you are aware, the basic concept for this project is ...

It is also possible to put this sort of expression to more devious uses. For instance, you can practice a subtle form of one-upmanship by implying that something unknown to your listeners is common knowledge to everyone else. You could say:

ご承知のように、最近の家電製品にはファジー理論が応用されております。

Goshōchi no yō ni, saikin no kaden-seihin ni wa fajī-riron ga ōyō sarete orimasu.

As you know, these days household appliances are incorporating the use of fuzzy logic.

or

ご存じの通り、3月に公定歩合が引き下げられました。

Gozonji no tōri, sangatsu ni kōtei-buai ga hikisagerare-mashita.

As you are aware, the bank rate was lowered in March.

Even though you're certain at least some of your listeners know nothing about your topic (they're the ones who are now squirming), you can be fairly sure none of them will pipe up and expose his ignorance.

Just to make sure I've got this right

念のためにお尋ねしますが……

Nen no tame ni otazune shimasu ga ...

Just to make sure I've got this right ...

There's never any harm in making sure. When you receive important information or instructions, it makes good sense to go over the essential points twice, even if you're pretty sure you got it right the first time. There's a ready-made phrase for this purpose:

念のためにお尋ねしますが……

Nen no tame ni otazune shimasu ga ...

Just to make sure I've got this right ...

It's particularly important to get repeat confirmation on easy-to-confuse items such as names, telephone numbers, dates and times, and figures and amounts—in fact, it's a cardinal rule of business. Here's how it's done:

念のためにお尋ねしますが、新宿支店ではなく
新橋支店ですね。

Nen no tame ni otazune shimasu ga, Shinjuku shiten de wa naku Shinbashi shiten desu ne.

Just to make sure I've got this right, it's the Shinbashi branch and not the Shinjuku branch, right?

or

念のためにお尋ねしますが、田中さんに電話す
ればよろしいんですね。

Nen no tame ni otazune shimasu ga, Tanaka-san ni denwa sureba yoroshii n' desu ne.

Just to make sure I've got it straight, it's Ms. Tanaka I'm supposed to call, right?

This is also a useful tactic to employ when you're told something that doesn't seem quite right. Maybe the other person misspoke or maybe you didn't hear what you thought you heard; in any case, you can put your doubts to rest by requesting confirmation. For instance:

念のためにお尋ねしますが、電話には私どもの
前川がでたんですね。

Nen no tame ni otazune shimasu ga, denwa ni wa watakushi-domo no Maekawa ga deta n' desu ne?

Just to make sure I've understood, it was Mr. Maekawa from our staff who spoke to you on the
phone, is that correct?

念のためにお尋ねしますが、お買いもとめにな
ったのは3月23日ですね。

*Nen no tame ni otazune shimasu ga, okaimotome ni
natta no wa sangatsu nijūsan-nichi desu ne.*

Just to make certain, the date of purchase was
March 23, is that correct?

When you're speaking to a valued customer, even if what
she's told you is utterly implausible (Mr. Maekawa retired
two years ago and the store was closed for a national holi-
day on March 23), you can't afford to alienate her by directly contradicting her version of events. By leading her
through the doubtful details a second time, you can give
her a chance to correct her own mistakes without having
to offend her by pointing them out. Still, if she sticks to
her dubious story, you may have to gently point out the
inconsistencies. You can use one of these phrases to broach
the issue:

私の思い違いかもしれませんが……

Watakushi no omoichigai ka mo shiremasen ga ...

It may be that I'm mistaken, but ...

ちょっと気になる点があるのですが……

Chotto ki ni naru ten ga aru no desu ga ...

There's one point that seems a bit curious ...

Did you like it?

ご満足いただけましたか。

Gomanzoku itadakemashita ka.

Did you like it?

A customer comes into the store and looks around. The clerk greets her with a polite but friendly:

いらっしゃいませ。

Irasshaimase.

Welcome.

The customer finds an item she likes—one of several blouses presented for her consideration by the clerk, who now urges her to try it on:

どうぞ、お試しください。

Dōzo, otameshi kudasai.

Please, go ahead and try it on.

The customer goes into the dressing room and tries on the blouse. Afterwards, when she comes back out looking pleased, the clerk immediately asks:

ご満足いただけましたか。お客様にぴったりで
　すよ。

*Gomanzoku itadakemashita ka. Okyaku-sama ni pittari
desu yo.*

Did you like it? It fits you perfectly.

or maybe

> いかがですか、お気に召しましたか。
>
> *Ikaga desu ka. Oki ni meshimashita ka.*
>
> How was it? Did you like it?

With these words, the clerk is creating an opening for some sociable chitchat. Naturally, she'll offer whatever advice or assistance she can with an eye to making a sale, but equally important is setting a friendly tone. All too many shops are staffed with clerks who apparently think nothing more is required of them than dead silence, occasionally punctuated by a brusque:

> お決まりでしょうか。
>
> *Okimari deshō ka.*
>
> All set?

If the customer appears to be having a hard time making up her mind, this clerk won't simply hover in the background trying to suppress her impatience. She'll say something like:

> こういうタイプがご希望ですか。よろしかった
> らいくつかお揃えしてみます。
>
> *Kō iu taipu ga gokibō desu ka. Yoroshikattara ikutsu ka
> osoroe shite mimasu.*
>
> Is this the type you're interested in? If you'd like, I
> can set out several for you to look over.

or

> 最近はこのタイプがよく出ています。
>
> *Saikin wa kono taipu ga yoku dete imasu.*
>
> This type is selling quite well these days.

or

> お客様のような方ですと、このタイプがよくお
> 似合いですね。
>
> *Okyaku-sama no yō na kata desu to, kono taipu ga
> yoku oniai desu ne.*
>
> You're the sort of person this type really looks nice
> on.

This clerk knows that while the quality of the product may be the customer's paramount concern, the attitude she conveys at the store has an extremely powerful influence on the decision to buy or not to buy. It's no coincidence that clerks who can communicate effectively with their customers also tend to be the ones posting the highest sales totals.

We'll give you a good price

> 勉強させていただきます。
>
> *Benkyō sasete itadakimasu.*
>
> We'll give you a good price.

If you've studied Japanese at all, you've undoubtedly come across the expression *benkyō suru* ("to study.") In the language of sales, however, this familiar phrase takes on another meaning entirely, as does its more polite and businesslike alternative form:

勉強させていただきます。

Benkyō sasete itadakimasu.

We'll give you a good price.

Another way to express the same meaning would be:

お安くしておきますよ。

Oyasuku shite okimasu yo.

We can let you have it cheap.

Apparently, however, the latter expression and others like it are disdained by those who sell and shop for higher-end merchandise. Like its English counterpart, the term *yasui* ("cheap")—along with the derivative forms *yasuku* and *oyasuku*—is considered either too prosaic or too earthy for the quality stuff, so the former expression is often preferred by hoity-toity clerks and clientele. No such scruples are to be found among the vendors of the traditional open marketplace, though: stroll through almost any one of them (or though the produce section in the basement of almost any department store) and you'll encounter a remarkably boisterous version of commerce that thrives on the chant:

安いよ！　安いよ！

Yasui yo! Yasui yo!

Cheap! Get it cheap!

Back at the big-ticket emporiums, they go in for a more genteel approach. A well-dressed fellow might quietly materialize at your side as you browse through the stock and remark in a discreetly modulated tone:

ただいまお買い得になっております。サービス
期間中ですので……

*Tadaima okaidoku ni natte orimasu. Sābisu kikan-chū
desu no de ...*

It's really quite a bargain at the moment. We're in
the middle of a sale, you see.

or

ご奉仕価格になっております。

Gohōshi kakaku ni natte orimasu.

That's a reduced price.

or

ご予算的にはこちらのほうがお得になっており
ます。

*Goyosan-teki ni wa kochira no hō ga otoku ni natte ori-
masu.*

This one has the merit of being less demanding on
one's budget.

The classic sales pitch at a typical high-priced store or
boutique might sound like this:

品質の点ではまずご心配はありませんし、この
お値段でしたらお買い物です。

*Hinshitsu no ten de wa mazu goshinpai wa arimasen
shi, kono onedan deshitara okaimono desu.*

You can be assured of the item's quality, and at
this price it's really a good buy.

The strategy behind the phraseology is transparent: the
clerk flatters you by suggesting your first concern is quality, rather than price, but he doesn't neglect to mention
that the price is right, too, just in case you happen to care.

Good morning

おはようございます。

Ohayō gozaimasu.

Good morning.

For people working in a typical office in Japan, and most particularly the younger employees, exaggerated displays of robust energy tend to be regarded in a very positive light. Some of these employees seem to assume that overt demonstrations of zeal are expected of them: you see plenty of office workers who have apparently taken a vow never to walk through the office—they run. One standard (and less exhausting) channel for the expression of a spunky attitude is the morning greeting:

おはようございます。

Ohayō gozaimasu.

Good morning.

With these words, often delivered at a surprisingly zesty volume, an employee greets everyone else at the office—the people he knows, including his superiors, as well as those he doesn't know—upon the first encounter of the morning. This is also the preferred way to greet people on the phone in the morning. An employee answering the phone at the trading firm Asahi Shōji would say:

おはようございます。アサヒ商事です。

Ohayō gozaimasu. Asahi Shōji desu.
Good morning, Asahi Shōji.

What makes *ohayō gozaimasu* a particularly favored greeting around the office is the second half of the phrase. The word *gozaimasu* (a humble variant of "to be") bespeaks modesty, respect, and a certain level of formality, and therefore carries just the right resonance for the businesslike environment of the workplace. By comparison, the standard greeting for post-morning encounters, *konnichi wa* ("hello"), and the evening greeting, *konban wa* ("good evening"), don't really cut it, especially when you're greeting the higher-ups; those phrases just don't have the sober, respectful ring of *ohayō gozaimasu*. So, how do you greet people when it gets to be lunch time or later—or don't you?

One school of thought recommends this approach to greeting a superior during the post-noon hours: bow your head while carefully intoning *konnichi wa* or *konban wa*. The overt gesture of respect and the less-than-formal greeting can combine, so the thinking goes, to convey a pleasing sense of polite familiarity.

Incidentally, in some circles *ohayō gozaimasu* (and the abbreviated version, *ohayō*) serves as the standard greeting for any time of day. This is an established custom in the cocktail trade and among entertainers and people in the arts, but many others have picked it up as well. For some students, the use of *ohayō* as an afternoon or evening greeting is reserved for close comrades—everyone else merely gets the time of day.

Good work

お疲れさまでした。
Otsukare-sama deshita.
Good work.

This phrase, one of the most commonly heard in the Japanese business world, conveys appreciative recognition of another person's labors. It could be used, for example, to greet a colleague returning to the office from an excursion to a client's factory in an outlying area; a more elaborate translation might be "Your hard work is appreciated." The figurative intention is to assuage the other person's fatigue and commend his exertions on the firm's behalf. A similar expression is:

ご苦労さまでした。
Gokurō-sama deshita.
Well done.

This one, however, is generally reserved for use by higher-ups addressing the people who serve under them and by older employees addressing their juniors. Strictly speaking, it would be a breach of etiquette for a younger employee or an underling to say *gokurō-sama deshita* to a senior colleague or boss—the one to use is *otsukare-sama deshita*. In less formal circumstances, the final word is often dropped from these expressions, yielding the abbreviated forms.

お疲れさま。

Otsukare-sama.

Good work.

and

ご苦労さま。

Gokurō-sama.

Well done.

The phrase *otsukare-sama deshita* is often employed as a form of farewell to a colleague or boss at the end of the work day. The following exchange between fellow employees features an everyday example of this sort of usage:

	お先に失礼いたします。
Sato-san:	*Osaki ni shitsurei itashimasu.*
	Pardon me, but I'm off.

	お疲れさまでした。
Kimura-san:	*Otsukare-sama deshita.*
	Good work today.

This sort of comradely send-off can help alleviate the stiffness that dominates the atmosphere in some offices.

Grammatically speaking, *otsukare-sama deshita* is a past-tense phrase. The present-tense form, *otsukare-sama desu*, is also used, but under different conditions—when the work in question is ongoing. Let's say a colleague, Mr. Horiguchi, is phoning in from outside the office (he's about to call on the publishing firm Dai-ichi Insatsu) to pick up his messages:

堀口です。いま第一印刷に向かっていますが、
何か連絡は入っていますか。

Horiguchi desu. Ima Dai-ichi Insatsu ni mukatte imasu ga, nani ka renraku wa haitte imasu ka.

This is Mr. Horiguchi. I'm on my way over to Dai-ichi Insatsu. Are there any messages for me?

You reply:

お疲れさまです。少々お待ちください。

Otsukare-sama desu. Shōshō omachi kudasai.

Good work. Just a moment, please. I'll check.

It's not quite what it should be

いまいちです。

Ima-ichi desu.

It's not quite what it should be.

If something doesn't quite meet your expectations, is just a bit lacking in some important quality, or simply doesn't work out in an entirely satisfactory manner, you can pronounce it *ima-ichi* ("not quite what it should be"). To get a sense of the way this expression is used around the office, consider this exchange between two colleagues:

新製品の売れ行きはどうかね。

Shinsei-hin no ureyuki wa dō ka ne.

How's the new product selling?

発売2週間目としては、いまいちですね。

Hatsubai·nishūkan-me toshite wa, ima-ichi desu ne.

Now·quite the way it should be, considering it's
been on the market for two weeks.

The term *ima-ichi* is a relative recent ersatz compound consisting of two components: *ima* ("now") and *ichi* ("one");
ima-hitotsu, another jury-rigged compound—*ima* + *hitotsu*
("one thing")—means the same thing and is used essentially the same way. Since *ima-ichi* conveys, in a literal sense,
the meaning that one thing is lacking at present, it is
considered by some speakers to be applicable only to that
which is regarded as a near miss, so analogous compounds
—*ima-ni*: *ima* + *ni* ("two"); *ima-san*: *ima* + *san* ("three")—
have been coined to indicate something farther off the
mark. The higher the number at the end, the greater the
sense of dissatisfaction or disappointment conveyed. Consider another brief exchange between colleagues:

ダイマル社のCM、評判はどうだろう。

Daimaru-sha no shīemu, hyōban wa dō darō.

What kind of reaction did that Daimaru TV com-
mercial get?

うーん、今二、いや今三かな。

Ūn, ima-ni, iya ima-san ka na.

Well, not that great—not great at all, actually.

Another shorthand expression you're likely to hear around
the office is *soku* ("right away"). This is probably not a
standard item in the vocabulary of a lot of native speakers of Japanese, who might be apt to use longer-estab-
lished expressions such as *sokkoku* ("immediately") or
tadachi ni ("right away"). Still, *soku* is an attention-getting

term when used in the context of work, as in this exchange between an employee and her section chief:

課長、新製品のプランがまとまりました。

Kachō, shinsei-hin no puran ga matomarimashita.

Chief, we've finished putting together the plans for the new product.

よし、即ミーティングだ。

Yoshi, soku mitingu da.

Okay, let's have a meeting right away.

Here's the boss, getting worked up about the fact that defective products are being sold and demonstrating another, somewhat different usage of *soku*:

なに、新製品に欠陥があった？　ばかな、欠陥
即発売停止じゃないか。

Nani, shinsei-hin ni kekkan ga atta? Baka na, kekkan soku hatsubai-teishi ja nai ka.

What, they found a defect in the new product! Of all the stupid ... A defect means you halt all sales immediately.

In the phrase *kekkan soku hatsubai-teishi* ("a defect means halting sales immediately"), the interposition of *soku* between *kekkan* ("defect") and *hatsubai-teishi* ("sales halt") conveys the sense of an automatic or immediate progression from the former to the latter: if the first thing happens then the second should immediately follow. We can presume everyone is supposed to know this, and that's why the irate boss recites the formula in this shorthand form.

This is just between us

ここだけの話ですが……

Koko dake no hanashi desu ga ...

This is just between us ...

Throughout the world, business people tend to treat information carefully, but it would be hard to imagine a business world more enamored of secrets than that of Japan. Still, wherever a lot of secrets are kept, almost as many are more than likely disclosed. In any case, when someone has confidential information to divulge, there are plenty of ready-made phrases to suit the occasion, such as:

ここだけの話ですが……

Koko dake no hanashi desu ga ...

This is just between us ...

Anytime someone starts off with a line like that, he can be confident he has won the attention of his audience. In business, after all, it's a point of pride to be able to anticipate events, to know what's going to happen before it happens (or at least before the competition finds out). So if what's about to be said has the forbidden-fruit appeal of confidential information, you can bet people will be listening. Here are some other phrases that can precede the spilling of the beans:

オフレコですが……

Ofu-reko desu ga ...

This can't be repeated, but ... (literally, This is off the record, but ...)

このことはまだ私と小野さんだけしか知らない ことですが……

Kono koto wa mada watashi to Ono-san dake shika shiranai koto desu ga ...

This is something that only Mr. Ono and I know about right now ...

どうかご内聞に願いますよ。

Dōka gonaibun ni negaimasu yo.

I'll have to ask you to keep this strictly confidential.

Of course, there's no guarantee that the information that follows will be anything of great importance, or even that it will be true. It tends not to matter—people pay attention anyway. But the one who lets the cat out of the bag had better not assume that his listeners will respect the confidence any more than he did. A secret disclosed is a secret no more, and the information can become common property in an amazingly short amount of time.

The attraction that confidential information holds, along with the tendency for "secrets" that have been divulged to rapidly become public knowledge, is well-known and is often shrewdly exploited for business purposes. Leaks can be planted to attract or divert attention, misinformation can be spread to throw rivals off the track, and confusion can be sown in the enemy camp, all under the guise of sharing otherwise private information. You might hear an exchange like this:

ここで話していいものかどうか……

Koko de hanashite ii mono ka dō ka ...

I'm not sure whether I should be saying this ...

誰にも話しませんから、聞かせてください。

Dare ni mo hanashimasen kara, kikasete kudasai.

I won't breath a word to anyone, so you can tell me.

Be careful. All may not be what it seems, and if you pass this secret along to others, you could be playing directly into the other guy's hands.

Thank you / I'm sorry / Pardon me

恐縮です。

Kyōshuku desu.

Thank you. / I'm sorry. / Pardon me.

One of the characteristic determiners of Japanese language usage is the speaker's gender. Some patterns and expressions are all but exclusively reserved for use by female speakers, others are for male speakers, and the rest—this is by far the biggest category—are for both. Another major influence on usage is the human predilection for ambiguity, which leads to the generation of multiple conventional interpretations of a single expression. Now then, here's a convenient phrase that exemplifies both of these aspects of usage:

恐縮です。

Kyōshuku desu.

Thank you. / I'm sorry. / Pardon me.

Often heard around the office, *kyōshuku desu* is regarded by many people, though not all, as a distinctly male-sounding phrase. In meaning, it's similar to this one:

恐れいります。

Osoreirimasu.

Excuse me. / I'm sorry.

The latter phrase, however, is not considered gender-specific and is probably just as commonly spoken by women as by men. Moreover, it doesn't cover quite the range of meanings and situations that *kyōshuku desu* does. A male employee can get a lot of mileage out of this one phrase, saying:

(when treated to dinner by the boss)

恐縮です。

Kyōshuku desu.

Thank you.

(after being reprimanded by a superior)

恐縮です。

Kyōshuku desu.

I'm sorry.

(when hauling a lot of luggage and making his way through a crowd)

恐縮ですが……

Kyōshuku desu ga ...

Pardon me ...

Versatile though it is, however, *kyōshuku desu* is in eminent danger of falling into disrepute due to overuse, and anyone who relies on this expression too much is likely to end up the butt of office jokes. A similar fate awaits those who overuse this familiar expression:

すみません。

Sumimasen.

Thank you. / I'm sorry. / Excuse me.

While this one can also be applied to a variety of situations, many people consider it distinctly inadequate as an expression of sincere gratitude or apology. For those purposes, these phrases are widely preferred:

ありがとうございます。

Arigatō gozaimasu.

Thank you very much.

申し訳ありません。

Mōshiwake arimasen.

I'm very sorry.

While it may seem the height of convenience to employ the same phrase for a whole variety of purposes, it's by no means necessarily advisable, lest you develop a reputation as someone of highly limited capabilities.

日本語ビジネス・フレーズ集
COMMON JAPANESE BUSINESS
PHRASES

1998年 6 月26日　第 1 刷発行

編　者　三省堂編修所

発行者　野間佐和子

発行所　講談社インターナショナル株式会社
　　　　〒112-8652 東京都文京区音羽 1-17-14
　　　　電話：03-3944-6493

印刷所　株式会社　平河工業社

製本所　株式会社　堅省堂

POWER JAPANESE SERIES
An ongoing series of compact, easy-to-use guides to essential language skills

ALL ABOUT KATAKANA
カタカナ練習ノート
Anne Matsumoto Stewart

Learn to read and write katakana in a quick, effective way by combining them into words.

Paperback, 144 pages; ISBN 4-7700-1696-4

ALL ABOUT PARTICLES
助詞で変わるあなたの日本語
Naoko Chino

The most common and less common particles brought together and broken down into some 200 usages, with abundant sample sentences.

Paperback, 128 pages; ISBN 4-7700-1501-1

ANIMAL IDIOMS
動物の慣用句集
Jeff Garrison and Masahiko Goshi

A memorable explanation of idioms—all dealing with animals. Organized by zoological category with background notes and sample sentences.

Paperback, 160 pages; ISBN 4-7700-1668-9

BASIC CONNECTIONS
Making Your Japanese Flow
日本語の基礎ルール
Kakuko Shoji

The connective expressions that facilitate the flow of ideas—how words and phrases dovetail, how clauses pair up with other clauses, and how sentences come together to create harmonious paragraphs.

Paperback, 154 pages; ISBN 4-7700-1968-8

BEYOND POLITE JAPANESE
A Dictionary of Japanese Slang and Colloquialisms
役にたつ話ことば辞典
Akihiko Yonekawa

Expressions that all Japanese, but few foreigners, know and use every day. Sample sentences for every entry.

Paperback, 176 pages; ISBN 4-7700-1539-9

"BODY" LANGUAGE
日本語の中の"ボディ"ランゲージ
Jeffrey G. Garrison

Common idioms that refer to the body through colorful colloquial expressions.

Paperback, 128 pages; ISBN 4-7700-1502-X

COMMON JAPANESE PHRASES
決まり文句の辞典
Compiled by Sanseido
Translated and Adapted by John Brennan

The appropriate words—fixed expressions and phrases for every social situation explained in short essay format, complete with tips on culture and alternatives.

Paperback, 144 pages; ISBN 4-7700-2072-4

COMMUNICATING WITH KI
The "Spirit" in Japanese Idioms
「気」の慣用句集
Jeff Garrison and Kayoko Kimiya

Over 200 idioms, all using the word ki, and all essential for communicating in Japanese.

Paperback, 144 pages; ISBN 4-7700-1833-9

FLIP, SLITHER, & BANG
Japanese Sound and Action Words
日本語の擬音語・擬態語
Hiroko Fukuda
Translated and edited by Tom Gally

The most common examples of onomatopoeia through sample sentences and situations—an excellent introduction to animated language.

Paperback, 128 pages; ISBN 4-7700-1684-0

HOW TO SOUND INTELLIGENT IN JAPANESE
A Vocabulary Builder
日本語の知的表現
Charles De Wolf

Lists, defines and gives examples for the vocabulary necessary to engage in intelligent conversations in fields such as politics, art, literature, business, and science.

Paperback, 144 pages; ISBN 4-7700-1747-2

INSTANT VOCABULARY
THROUGH PREFIXES AND SUFFIXES
増えて使えるヴォキャブラリー
Timothy J. Vance

Expand vocabulary and improve reading comprehension by modifying your existing lexicon.

Paperback, 128 pages; ISBN 4-7700-1500-3

JAPANESE VERBS AT A GLANCE
日本語の動詞
Naoko Chino

Clear and straightforward explanations of Japanese verbs—their functions, forms, roles, and politeness levels.

Paperback, 180 pages; ISBN 4-7700-1985-8

KANJI IDIOMS
四字熟語
*George Wallace
and Kayoko Kimiya*

Frequently used phrases composed of four kanji characters essential for educated conversation.

Paperback, 160 pages; ISBN 4-7700-1943-2

LIVING JAPANESE
A Modern Reader
楽しく読む日本語
Marc Bookman and Kazuko Fujii

A selection of short fiction and non-fiction articles in Japanese with vocabulary lists, idiomatic expressions and quizzes.

Paperback, 132 pages; ISBN 4-7700-2035-X

LOVE, HATE AND AND EVERYTHING IN BETWEEN
Expressing Emotions in Japanese
日本語の感情表現集
Mamiko Murakami
Translated by **Ralph McCarthy**

All the vocabulary and phrases necessary to hit just the right nuance and say exactly what you feel.

Paperback, 170 pages; ISBN 4-7700-2089-9

MAKING SENSE OF JAPANESE
What the Textbooks Don't Tell You
日本語の秘訣
Jay Rubin

Answers to all those nagging questions of basic Japanese, masterfully handled with a light touch and a good deal of humor. Formerly published as *Gone Fishin'*, now with a new chapter on upside-down sentences.

Paperback, 140 pages; ISBN 4-7700-2310-3

READ REAL JAPANESE
日本語で読もう
Janet Ashby

Ten essays by popular Japanese authors. All vocabulary is defined, and grammar explained so the book can be read without a dictionary.

Paperback, 168 pages; ISBN 4-7700-1754-5

STRANGE BUT TRUE
A True-Life Japanese Reader
デキゴトロジーを読む
Tom Gally

Eight real-life stories packed with humor and oddity. An entertaining introduction to reading Japanese.

Paperback, 140 pages; ISBN 4-7700-2057-0

T-SHIRT JAPANESE VERSUS NECKTIE JAPANESE
Two Levels of Politeness
Tシャツの日本語ネクタイの日本語
Hiroko Fukuda
Translated by **Charles De Wolf**

Paired dialogues expressing the same thoughts demonstrate polite and colloquial language, complete with down-to-earth commentary.

Paperback, 152 pages; ISBN 4-7700-1834-7

The best-selling language course is now even better!

JAPANESE FOR BUSY PEOPLE Revised Edition

改訂版　コミュニケーションのための日本語　全3巻

Association for Japanese-Language Teaching (AJALT)

The leading textbook for conversational Japanese has been improved to make it easier than ever to teach and learn Japanese.

- Transition to advancing levels is more gradual.
- Kana version available for those who prefer Japanese script. Audio supplements compatible with both versions.
- English-Japanese glossary added to each volume.
- Short kanji lessons introduced in Volume II.
- Clearer explanations of grammar.
- Shorter, easy-to-memorize dialogues.

Volume I

Teaches the basics for communication and provides a foundation for further study.

- Additional appendices for grammar usage.

Text	paperback, 232 pages	ISBN 4-7700-1882-7
Text / Kana Version	paperback, 256 pages	ISBN 4-7700-1987-4
Tapes	three cassette tapes (total 120 min.)	ISBN 4-7700-1883-5
Compact Discs	two CD's (total 120 min.)	ISBN 4-7700-1909-2
Workbook	paperback, 184 pages	ISBN 4-7700-1907-6
Workbook Tapes	two cassette tapes (total 100 min.)	ISBN 4-7700-1769-3
Japanese Teacher's Manual	paperback, 160 pages	ISBN 4-7700-1906-8
English Teacher's Manual	paperback, 244 pages	ISBN 4-7700-1888-6

Volume II

Provides the basic language skills necessary to function in a professional environment.

Text	paperback, 288 pages	ISBN 4-7700-1884-3
Text / Kana Version	paperback, 296 pages	ISBN 4-7700-2051-1
Tapes	three cassette tapes (total 200 min.)	ISBN 4-7700-1885-1
Compact Discs	three CD's (total 200 min.)	ISBN 4-7700-2136-4

Workbook	paperback, 260 pages	ISBN 4-7700-2037-6
Workbook Tapes	three cassette tapes (total 130 min.)	ISBN 4-7700-2111-9
Japanese Teacher's Manual	paperback, 168 pages	ISBN 4-7700-2036-8

Volume III

Expands vocabulary and structure to bring the student to the intermediate level.

Text	paperback, 248 pages	ISBN 4-7700-1886-X
Text / Kana Version	paperback, 296 pages	ISBN 4-7700-2052-X
Tapes	three cassette tapes (total 200 min.)	ISBN 4-7700-1887-8
Compact Discs	three CD's (total 200 min.)	ISBN 4-7700-2137-2
Japanese Teacher's Manual	paperback, 200 pages	ISBN 4-7700-2306-5

Kana Workbook

Straightforward text for quick mastery of hiragana and katakana utilizing parallel learning of reading, writing, listening and pronunciation.

• Grids for writing practice.
• Reading and writing exercises.
• Optional audio tape aids in pronunciation.

| Text | paperback, 80 pages | ISBN 4-7700-2096-1 |
| Tape | one cassette tape (40 min.) | ISBN 4-7700-2097-X |

JAPANESE FOR PROFESSIONALS
ビジネスマンのための実戦日本語
Association for Japanese-Language Teaching (AJALT)

A serious and detailed manual of the language of trade, commerce, and government. Fourteen lessons introduce common business situations with key sentences and a dialogue to illustrate proper usage.

paperback, 256 pages ISBN 4-7700-2038-4

KODANSHA INTERNATIONAL DICTIONARIES

Easy-to-use dictionaries designed for non-native learners of Japanese.

KODANSHA'S FURIGANA JAPANESE-ENGLISH DICTIONARY

ふりがな和英辞典

The essential dictionary for all students of Japanese.
• Furigana readings added to all kanji
• Comprehensive 16,000-word basic vocabulary

Vinyl binding, 592 pages; ISBN 4-7700-1983-1

KODANSHA'S FURIGANA ENGLISH-JAPANESE DICTIONARY

ふりがな英和辞典

The companion to the essential dictionary for all students of Japanese.
• Furigana readings added to all kanji
• Comprehensive 14,000-word basic vocabulary

Vinyl binding, 728 pages; ISBN 4-7700-2055-4

KODANSHA'S ROMANIZED JAPANESE-ENGLISH DICTIONARY

ローマ字和英辞典

A portable reference written for beginning and intermediate students.
• 16,000-word vocabulary.
• No knowledge of kanji necessary.

Vinyl binding, 688 pages; ISBN 4-7700-1603-4

KODANSHA'S COMPACT KANJI GUIDE

常用漢英熟語辞典

A functional character dictionary that is both compact and comprehensive.
• 1,945 essential *joyo kanji*.
• 20,000 common compounds.
• Three indexes for finding kanji.

Vinyl binding, 928 pages; ISBN 4-7700-1553-4